Secret Gardens of Aotearoa

Secret Gardens of Aotearoa

Field Notes & Practical Wisdom

Jane Mahoney
& Sophie Bannan

Photography by Jane Mahoney,
Josephine Meachen & Sophie Bannan

For Harriet

CONTENTS

Introduction	7
Ngā Kaupeka	12
Crosshill Garden	40
Hakea	70
Violet's Garden	96
Wellington Garden	120
Birch Hill Flower Farm	142
Cornwall Pocket Farm	164
Texture Garden	190
Greenhills Paradise	214
Bush Retreat	234
The Little Insect Farm	264
Fantail and Flax	288
Acknowledgements	315
Further Reading	316
Photography Credits	317
About the Authors	319

INTRODUCTION

As it has for many gardeners, my own gardening journey has been full of steep learning curves, revelations, failures, breakthroughs and gardening heroes — whose shared wisdom contributes to my ongoing accumulation of skills and knowledge. It has also been defined by where I've lived and stages of my life — from raising three children with little time to garden, to growing herbs and tomatoes in pots on a central-city balcony, and now tending a one-acre hillside property on Banks Peninsula. The concept of the Secret Gardens website came to me four years into this garden transformation.

Prior to taking on our Banks Peninsula property, I had little knowledge of native plants. Wanting to stay true to what would have originally grown in this bay before the bush was cleared for farming involved much research, creating plant lists and buying 'eco-sourced' plants from local specialist nurseries. The Lyttelton Harbour property on a steep hillside had been planted with some native trees in the 1980s, then largely neglected for twenty years, so using native planting to improve the biodiversity and create habitats and food sources for native birds and lizards was the foundation of my planning.

My plan involved clearing out all the 'weed' trees — blackberry and invasive muehlenbeckia — and establishing different garden areas, including a permaculture orchard and tiered vegetable garden. Paths and steps needed building to create access, and cleared trees became mulch to improve water retention and soil quality. Over this time I was also learning about the principles of permaculture, about planning an orchard to ensure an extended harvest period and about soil health.

Concurrently, I gardened at the Millhouse — a wholly contrasting garden surrounding an 1870s cottage on the Canterbury Plains. The one-acre property has been in our family since I was a child and I have gardened there for many years, applying new knowledge I acquired whilst maintaining its established exotic trees, orchard and Victorian cottage-style garden.

Long hours spent in the garden also gave time for thinking, and the threads of observations and ideas that grew into Secret Gardens began coming together. Whilst the solitary nature of gardening pursuits is part of its appeal, I had always loved calling on my mother for advice, or visiting other people's gardens for inspiration and to expand my plant knowledge. Often, though, the types of gardens that open to the public are of a scale unattainable to most of us, and I frequently found myself peering over someone's gate, wishing I could explore their wild suburban garden. Reflecting on how much I had learnt over the past few years, I began envisaging the vast pool of knowledge held by 'home gardeners' and what an incredible resource that would amount to — their gardens living testaments to their lifetimes of knowledge accumulation.

In 2021, with the support of my daughter Sophie (co-author of this book), photographer Josephine Meachen and our founding team of garden hosts, secretgardens.co.nz was launched. I created Secret Gardens as a platform for sharing this knowledge. The website features a curated selection of home gardens across Aotearoa, each with an experienced gardener passionate about sharing their wisdom by hosting guided visits and workshops in their own garden.

Not all the gardens in this book are featured on the website, but they do all embody our values of sustainable gardening practices, tuning in, learning through observation and, of course, sharing knowledge. The gardens have been selected for their diversity in gardening styles and for their creators — humble home gardeners, who have each developed a wealth of knowledge over their lifetime and have generously contributed their practical wisdom to *Secret Gardens of Aotearoa*.

The growing interest in gardening gives me great optimism for a present and future that prioritises resourcefulness, food security, biodiversity and 'living lightly'. I hope you enjoy exploring the gardens in this book and find renewed inspiration and community in your own gardening practice.

— Jane Mahoney, founder of Secret Gardens

NGĀ KAUPEKA

Ngā Kaupeka (The Seasons) is an urban organic garden in Forrest Hill on Auckland's North Shore. Since buying the 703-square-metre property in 2010, Phoebe and Dave have designed and built productive, functional and recreational spaces, including an abundant kitchen garden and a mini-orchard. They have chickens, composting systems and a propagation shed.

In a council reserve just around the corner from their property, Phoebe and Dave instigated Grow Forrest Hill, a community garden that produces organic food, connecting their community in the process. Neighbouring the local kindergarten, a playground and sports field, the once bare section is now a beautiful space of raised planter boxes brimming with vegetables and flowers, and buzzing with bees.

For Phoebe and Dave, gardening is a powerful force for good in the community. When Dave looks at the tītoki — which they planted as 60-centimetre saplings and are now two storeys high — he thinks about their long journey to parenthood, and how building their garden carried them through.

Gardening is an inherently paradoxical activity. It means existing at the point of tension between being and doing, between accepting the majesty and might of nature, and striving to imprint a human hand upon the earth. To plant a seed is to hope and to invest, but to avoid going entirely mad, this has to be done with an acknowledgement of the fact there are no guarantees. And that we can only do so much. The movement of a garden sets it aside from other art forms; no stasis is ever reached, there is no 'finished'.

— GRACE ALEXANDER, *GROW AND GATHER*

ABOUT THE GARDENERS

Phoebe and Dave's gardening practice is deeply entwined with their family and community. Twelve years on from purchasing their Forrest Hill property, the garden and their gardening ideology have expanded to include a seedling stand as well as the community garden. Their two beautiful children are involved in every aspect.

For as long as Phoebe can remember, she's been drawn to gardens. If she ever came across some kind of structured productive space, she gravitated there. Her early years were spent on a classic quarter-acre (1012-square metre) section in semi-rural Bethlehem, Tauranga, with mature vegetation, chickens and a vegetable garden to feed the family. With three older siblings and a small-town locale, Phoebe was a 'free-range kid' whose patch extended beyond the fence to exploring the nearby valley.

Later, when Phoebe's family moved between Auckland and Wellington, she saw her parents landscape a couple of different gardens to meet their changing needs. This gave her an appreciation of the intentionality of gardening: she realised that plants don't just happen around you. The understanding that your garden could be purposefully created has been central to her own gardening journey.

When she finished high school, Phoebe found herself undecided about her next move. She had enjoyed working for a florist while at school, and her parents were keen for her to pursue what she loved, so Phoebe enrolled in Unitec's Sustainable Horticulture programme. The course gave her hands-on skills and confidence in gardening, but at that time she didn't see a future in horticulture beyond working in a garden centre. She transferred to a town-planning degree at Auckland University, bringing her expanding horticultural knowledge with her, and also began digging up lawns at her student flats to plant productive gardens.

The pōhutukawa tree in Dave's childhood garden extends over three properties. It's the kind of tree that inspires passing arborists to knock on the door and request a closer look. Dave and his three older siblings grew up in the branches of this magnificent tree, and gorged themselves on fruit from the orchard of their Takapuna home. As a young man Dave was more interested in skating than gardening, but as a designer he likes to create spaces, and when he met Phoebe their interests merged.

Phoebe and Dave bought their Forrest Hill property — a classic suburban bungalow with a sparse, grassed section — as a home for their future family. Their desire for children unfolded into the ordeal of infertility, a process heavy with the grief of facing a future they could not control. Their garden became a mechanism for healing as they got stuck into a project they hoped would one day be enjoyed by their children. The garden was a hopeful space for them, pulling them forward through the seasons, rewarding them with growth, and connecting them with a like-minded gardening community.

Deciding to go down the path of adoption, Phoebe and Dave embarked on a year-long process of workshops and social-worker visits, all the while pinching themselves that maybe their future would hold children after all. Then one day they received a call from their social worker — a baby boy had just been born, and his birth mother had chosen Phoebe and Dave to be his parents. The call came on a Monday, and the rest of the week was a whirlwind. Friends rallied around, Phoebe quit her job, and by Friday they were home with Harley, learning to be a family.

A few years later baby Kyla joined them, and their family is now complete. Both adoptions are open, so Phoebe and Dave's family tree is grafted together, with many branches wrapped around them and their children.

It wasn't the biological family Phoebe and Dave had set out to create their garden for, but the adventure taught them that life can take you in surprising directions that are every bit as beautiful and rewarding as the path you had planned. It is a blessing they don't take for granted.

Harley and Kyla have grown up in the garden. Three-year-old Kyla toddles around the garden in her yellow gummies, observing monarch butterflies, cuddling the chooks, and eating raspberries straight from the bush. She watches intently as Phoebe plants seedlings in the raised beds, letting Kyla water them in with her pail — and gives the dogs a drench for good measure!

Seven-year-old Harley is gentle, observant and hands-on in every aspect of the garden, rewarding Phoebe's incredible patience for getting her children involved. Both are confident and gain palpable joy from making real contributions. Harley feeds the chooks and collects eggs, and can often be found sporting his beekeeping suit or with a cordless drill in hand.

With the home garden brimming with trees, vegetables, flowers, chickens and children, Phoebe and Dave began work on setting up the community garden. The project began with a free seedling stand on the street outside their house, to which people in the neighbourhood began adding. A bare patch of council reserve next to the local kindy caught their eye and, after a long process of council applications and community consultation, permission was granted and Grow Forrest Hill became a reality.

That Phoebe and Dave find the energy to manage the community garden on top of their full lives is reflective of their approach to both gardening and life: the more you give, the more your capacity for giving grows.

ABOUT THE GARDEN

The first thing Phoebe and Dave did when they bought their place was plant trees: native tītoki, puka, manatu (ribbonwood), nīkau, tī kōuka (cabbage trees) and mānuka, and a small orchard at the rear of the house. They got stuck into landscaping straight away, but not without a plan.

As a starting point, they recognised that their section lent itself to having several different zones — the house is in the middle with space at the front, at the sides and at the back. Phoebe knew she wanted an orchard with chickens, a vegetable garden, classic flat lawn for the kids to play on, and an entertaining space with an outdoor fire.

Gardening in a low-lying valley with heavy clay soil certainly has its challenges. In the early stages a lot of the trees and planting struggled and some died. The solution has been a long process of building up the soil and finding the right spots for the right plants. They spent years observing other Auckland gardens, saving pages from magazines, and taking note of council planting of natives in public spaces. Many of the landscaping ideas and plant combinations they saw have been directly replicated in their own plan. That's always their advice to people who don't know where to start — open your eyes up to public spaces, look at what they've planted and what's thriving, take note of the details, take photos of things you like.

While they have brought complementary skills to the project — Dave the landscaper and Phoebe the gardener — tensions do sometimes arise when their approaches clash. Phoebe is a self-confessed hoarder, always on the lookout for new ideas and materials that could be put to use, making decisions as she goes, and approaching the garden as an evolving project. Whereas Dave, with his design background and aesthetic, likes to work to a plan. For him there are always thousands of options, so a plan is the materialisation of intentional decisions, of ideas narrowed down to what will best fit their purpose.

The front section of the property is planted primarily with natives, with lawn and an entertaining area. Set on a spacious wooden deck extending from the house, a large dining table, sheltered by a ceiling of grapevines, is the social hub. An adjacent outdoor fire provides warmth and ambient lighting for late-night dinner parties, and Dave's prized skate ramp descends from the back of the deck.

The garden at the rear of the house is in two parts. On one side is Phoebe's structured, tidy potager garden, and the other side is wild, lovely chaos. Phoebe has always been drawn to the formal potager-style vegetable garden, remembering the raised beds and white chip of a garden she visited as a child with her mum.

Ngā Kaupeka's raised beds are edged with massive sleepers salvaged from the Seafarers' Building demolition site. The handsome white chip paths double as mud control for the low-lying bog-prone section. Behind the vegetable garden is a glasshouse, built by Dave using recycled window frames.

A flower bed — one of Phoebe's non-negotiables in the garden plan — separates the meticulous, productive vegetable garden from the orchard, which is the perfect kind of chaotic, with compost bins, chooks, a bug hotel (built by Harley) and wildflowers under fruit trees. This is not just the space for the messy work of an extensive composting operation, but is an un-precious space for Harley and Kyla to do anything they like — from making mud pies to building huts and climbing trees.

GROW FORREST HILL

At inductions for new members, Dave reiterates that Forrest Hill Community Garden is not about the plants and produce, it's about doing something together, about learning, and about connecting with one another. Gardening is a great leveller. No matter what stage of life you're at, when you come together and garden side by side you are all on the same page. It's a beautiful catalyst for creating community because the focus is always on the task at hand, and the connection is an inevitable by-product.

The idea for the community garden surfaced in about 2019 when Harley started kindy. Phoebe and Dave had always been keen on the concept, but

it was a chance conversation with kindergarten staff that was the lightbulb moment for Phoebe. She came home and told Dave about the nearby council space, he googled 'how to start a community garden', and so the project began.

Nothing about the process was straightforward, however. Dave enthusiastically describes it as a complicated, time-consuming, obstacle-laden path that required a change of land use application under the Reserves Act and the formation of a charitable trust. They needed to arrange insurance, devise a health and safety plan and a garden plan, and consult with the community.

The process ground on, the plan was changed twice to accommodate various parties' requests, and presented twice to the local board. Council permission to start the community garden was finally forthcoming . . . just as the first Covid-19 lockdown hit.

With the project on hold, and recognising an increased interest in gardening while everyone was working from home, Phoebe created a stand on their front berm from which she could give away surplus seedlings. Dave designed and built the stand from old pallets, with a blackboard for announcements. People helped themselves to seedlings, Phoebe added more, and it quickly became a (socially distanced) community hub. People would stop and chat over the fence, and soon began dropping off their own seedlings, along with surplus produce, houseplants, cuttings and even landscaping materials.

For Phoebe, the produce stand and community garden embody the spirit of reciprocal generosity and community that gardening generates. The humble act of gifting excess plant cuttings or produce is an expression of generosity that is counter to our consumerist world. It's an act that is microcosmic of Phoebe and Dave's whole approach to gardening — an ideology of generosity, intentionality and community building.

The seedling stand now occupies a spot across the road, next to their thriving community garden. Every weekend a whole range of locals gather to work on the garden. Harley takes charge of gardening days, having been encouraged to be actively involved at every stage. He takes enormous pride in what he has achieved alongside his family and community. The produce is shared among the gardeners and beyond.

There are workshops and fundraising events, and the most recent development has been the setting-up of a community composting hub. The commercial-grade, rodent-proof bins are designed and made in

New Zealand by The CarbonCycle Company, and anyone can contribute their organic household waste.

As busy as they are, Phoebe and Dave describe gardening as their downtime. It's about physical, mental, social and spiritual health, about changing pace. They have a to-do list, and each weekend they decide the priority tasks and projects. It's never a chore (except for maybe pruning the 8-metre-high tītoki!).

Phoebe and Dave describe Ngā Kaupeka as 80 per cent finished, with the remainder of their vision being an ever-evolving project. They see gardening, and life, not as a series of jobs or tasks to get through, but as affording joy in every aspect: being together in the garden, finding solutions, moving through the seasons, and inviting people into their lives. Most joyous and rewarding of all, though, is sharing their garden with their children.

NOTES FROM PHOEBE

OUR GLASSHOUSE/POTTING SHED

The idea of a glasshouse always seemed to me like a bit of a garden luxury — the ultimate gardener's accessory. The prospect of being able to, for example, grow tomatoes all year round was typical of the grand plan I had initially.

My original inspiration was one I spotted online, belonging to Auckland couple Lucy and Stephen Marr. So began a year-long journey salvaging old windows from builder mates and roadside inorganic collections.

Dave designed the structure carefully and says it was like a giant jigsaw, with different shapes and sizes to fit together. Visually, the end result was all that I had imagined. However, on a practical level, I quickly came to realise that the space we had created, with its draughty gaps and non-transparent/solid green roof (covered in succulents salvaged from a friend's wedding), made it more suited to a cosy retreat-come-potting shed than a light, bright hot-box.

I have come to love that potting shed as much as anything else in my garden. To have a dedicated space to sow seeds, transplant seedlings, propagate cuttings and store all the ingredients to do the above instantly, *is* a garden luxury. As for that hot-box — I now have a much smaller cold frame that Dave has built from a large recycled window, which serves the purpose of extending the seasons for growing seedlings (for the home garden and the community garden).

+++

OUR APPROACH TO PLANNING CROP ROTATION

We practise crop rotation for the health of the soil, and for seasonal interest in the garden. The summer rotation runs from the end of September to the beginning of March, and the winter from late March to early September (see below).

I try to follow the principle that 'givers' (e.g. legumes) are followed by 'high feeders' (e.g. Solanaceae, cucurbits, brassicas), followed by 'low feeders' (e.g. roots and alliums).

But the soil is very forgiving. The overall aim is to avoid planting the same thing in the same space year after year, so any crop movement is good.

Our garden receives low sunlight levels in winter, so recently we have incorporated green manures (e.g. broad beans, lupins) into the winter rotation, the principle being that less productive growth is less disappointing if the point is to feed the soil rather than us!

NGĀ KAUPEKA

PROCESSING FOOD WASTE IN AN URBAN HOUSEHOLD

Our goal is to generate close to zero organic kerbside waste. With a view to building up the soil and making our own seed-raising mix, anything biodegradable is seen as an input for the compost system. Compost inputs need to be about 50:50 nitrogen source (kitchen scraps, lawn clippings etc) and carbon source (autumn leaves, cardboard, paper/compostable packaging).

Our compost system has four components:

1. Compost bins

Compost bins are the foundational component of our food/organic waste system. We have a two-bay/bin system — one for collecting, while the other is 'cooking'. An essential part of this is a kitchen scraps caddy — in our case a lidded 'bread tin' that fits inside the opening of the now-unused waste disposal machine. This means the bench or chopping board can be wiped straight in.

We make two hot composts a year, in autumn and spring. 'Green' nitrogen inputs that have been collecting in one bin are layered with 'brown' carbon inputs until the bin is full. It is then covered with coffee sacks (and a tarpaulin in winter) and left for a week to start the heating ('cooking') process, then aerated every week or two over the following eight weeks. To aerate, I stab the pile with a sawn-off golf club — right through to the bottom 20 or so times. Ideally it is then left to cure for another 6–8 weeks, but it can be used as a mulch at this point.

2. Bokashi

A bokashi bin that lives in our laundry is great for dealing with scraps that can be problematic in attracting rodents if put straight in the compost — for example meat, dairy products and bread. It's also great for reducing the number of trips to the compost bin in winter! A bucket of buried bokashi is a really effective addition to the cooking compost bin, acting as an activator and giving the existing microbes a good boost. We have two (20-litre) bins, so one is filling while the other is fermenting.

3. Worm farm

Worm farms are more a means of growing fertiliser than processing food waste, as they use a lot less than compost bins. We utilise in-ground worm farms — 10-litre lidded buckets with holes drilled in that are buried in the raised beds. We also have a larger Hungry Bin worm farm from which we collect the leachate to use as a liquid fertiliser, and the worm castings to add to potting mix. Like pets, the worms are fed their preferred foods with care — fruit and vegetable scraps only (e.g. left-over coleslaw, salad, fruit cores and peels), cut small to speed up processing.

4. Chickens

Chickens are the jewels in the compost crown, orchestrating their own perfect circular system. They live in the orchard where the compost bins are situated. The bins have removable slats at the front so they rise with the level of the compost. During the day I remove the cover and let the chickens hop in and scratch around in the top layer. They eat the kitchen and garden waste, while their scratching aerates the compost, and their manure adds to the mix. It also makes an ideal fertiliser for the fruit trees when they scratch around the orchard. They then produce eggs, an ideal food source for us! The end result of this organic waste process is a compost that's like black gold — a valuable addition to the vegetable gardens and an ingredient for making potting mix — perfect for transplanting seedlings.

+++

PHOEBE'S POTTING MIX

2 parts sieved compost
2 parts coconut coir
1 part pumice sand
¼ part worm castings

Mix in a big container and keep covered to prevent it drying out — a coffee sack works well.

+++

BUILDING A COMMUNITY PRODUCE/SEEDLING STAND

Materials
To keep the cost down we used free pallet wood, cutting the lengths with a circular saw. You can also do this with a hand saw if you are up for a workout.

Method
Start by building two identical A-frames. These will set the height of the stand. Ours is 2 metres tall, as this provides room to stand under the roof.

Using a level, mark on each leg the desired position of each shelf. The measurement between the front and back frame legs will give you the depth of each shelf. Build your shelves based on these dimensions. Note that the width will be the same for all shelves, but the depth will vary. Screw a sheet of ply underneath each frame to form the base of the shelf.

Build the roof, making it a bit wider so it covers the ends of the frame. You can choose the depth you like, but matching it to the lowest shelf is a good starting point. Instead of lining it with ply, cut individual lengths of the pallet wood and nail or screw these to the top.

Attach the shelves to the frame at a slight angle, sloping forwards to allow for greater visibility from the road for passers-by to see what's on offer. Drill drainage holes every 5 centimetres along the lowest point of each shelf to allow water to run out. You might also want to screw L-brackets under each shelf to improve the rigidity of the structure.

Hang a sign on the back. We used lengths of chain, and painted a spare piece of ply with blackboard paint. Then let your creative blackboard art skills flow!

CROSSHILL GARDEN

Nestled into the gentle eastern slopes of Mt Maude, just south of Lake Hāwea in Central Otago's lakes district, is Crosshill, an established garden set among century-old trees. The massive native beech, birch and flowering cherry trees stand as a testament to the foresight of the property's first gardeners.

Crosshill was established as a sheep station in one of the area's early agricultural settlements; the original woolshed now serves as the potting shed and flower-drying area.

Between the rocky under-bed of its mountainous setting and pockets of rich, fertile soil redolent of its farming days, the range of the garden's soil is as extreme as the Central Otago seasons. This is both the coldest and driest region of New Zealand, with hot summers and harsh winters. Early Māori primarily occupied the area seasonally by way of routes through the Nevis Valley from the south and the Clutha River from the north.

We all pass on, our gardens change, many disintegrate and disappear. That is not important. What matters is the continuing cycle of sharing and learning about plants, and perhaps a little bit of us remains with our plants.

— BETH CHATTO, *BETH CHATTO'S WOODLAND GARDEN: SHADE-LOVING PLANTS FOR YEAR-ROUND INTEREST*

ABOUT THE GARDENER

When Ali took an evening woodwork class in Christchurch in the early 1980s, she built a planter box. She and husband Nic had recently relocated from Australia, and to supplement their meagre student incomes Ali began growing leafy greens out the back of their flat. This was her first dabble in gardening since obtaining her Brownies gardener badge in the UK where she grew up.

Ali can trace her interest in gardening back to her grandfather, who provided food for the family, all grown on his small Luton townhouse section. It was the immediate postwar period, so his gardening was practical and very much out of necessity. He raised all his seedlings in a glasshouse that was always brimming with growth — a place of wonder for little Ali.

As well as all the vegetables they needed, her grandfather grew flowers and made compost. With no car, there was no 'popping down to the garden shop', so the garden was self-sufficient — a closed system that fed the land to feed the family. The only exception was horse poo left by the milk delivery cart, which Ali's grandmother would race out and collect with a spade to add to the garden.

Times were so tight that often the family could not afford meat, so the garden was essential to sustain the family. Ali recalls the story of when her mother's pet bunny became winter stew . . .

Her grandfather's garden is a formative memory for Ali, but it would be many years and many gardens before she felt she'd gained the knowledge and experience to call herself a gardener.

She and Nic bought their first home in Invercargill — on a quarter-acre section with a glasshouse. These days, Ali is an avid reader of gardening

books, but back then she slowly acquired knowledge and skills through trial and error.

Southland conditions were sympathetic though — Ali recalls that you could put anything in the ground and it would grow. In their second home, and now with two young children, Ali had less time but more reason to grow her gardening knowledge. It was here, with her children in tow, that she first implemented crop rotation in a gridded vegetable garden, and learnt about composting.

The garden wasn't big but it was productive and had a few established fruit trees, so pruning was added to her growing skill base. Ali laid a brick path while her children played in the sandpit (when they weren't raiding the gooseberry bushes). As the years went on, Ali grew more and more vegetables to feed her growing family, and propagated 173 roses from cuttings.

When they moved from Southland to Central Otago, Ali had her first opportunity to build a garden from scratch. Memories of her grandfather's garden, that first wooden planter box she made, her various gardens in Southland and the growing impulse to feed her family all came together in this new garden — and for the first time Ali really felt like she knew what she was doing. She could improve the soil, care for fruit trees, produce an abundance of vegetables, and work with the local conditions and seasons.

Ali went big. Her 4 × 4-metre raised beds were interspersed with central arches that supported tall, compact Ballerina apple trees. Inspired by Monet's garden at Giverny, the orchard surrounding the vegetable garden was underplanted in pollinators — peonies and garlic. She planted grapevines, an asparagus patch, and a hedge to provide shelter from the wind.

Ali remembers collecting her daughter from the bus stop after school and spending hours in the vegetable garden with her, perched on the edge of a planter bed, grazing on fresh peas and catching up on the day's news. They spent 12 years at this property, the children growing up among the garden spaces Ali created, and rolling their eyes at the nightly reminder that, just a moment ago, their dinner had been growing in the garden.

More of an ideology than a specific plan, Ali's approach to gardening is practical, meditative and constantly responsive to the changing environment and needs of her family. She learns through observing and doing — gardening to the conditions rather than fighting against them. Right plant, right place. When an area Ali thought would be perfect for dahlias proved too dry, she moved them the following season. Observing that bearded irises were thriving in a certain area of the garden, she set about dividing them up and extending the path to the part where she now sells the gorgeous blooms and rhizomes at the gate. This flexible approach has guided her through the successes and challenges of gardening over the years.

Ali devours gardening books and magazines, and could watch Monty Don in *Gardeners' World* for days on end. She and Nic have visited gardens around the world and always find something different in each of them: the romance of Monet's Impressionist garden at Giverny, the gargantuan scale of Versailles, the sensory late mediaeval/Moorish Alhambra Palace gardens in Spain.

Ali's favourite gardens are ones in which she can feel the gardener guiding her through the spaces they have created. An interest in history, especially social history, inspires her garden pilgrimages, as well as informing her wider gardening interests. She is driven by the idea of gardening the 'old way' — her grandfather is always on her shoulder, whispering practical advice, connecting her to her family history and reminding her why she does what she does — to feed her family.

As if to prove the point, her most valued inheritance from her grandfather is a little steel widger, a tool for pricking out seedlings. She's had it since her gardening journey began.

ABOUT THE GARDEN

Crosshill is an eclectic garden that includes the original rose garden, an orchard that is being transformed into a food forest, a newly created woodland garden, a propagation and potting shed, a picking garden for the roadside flower stall, a tea garden and an extensive vegetable garden.

It's quite a new project for Ali — she and Nic bought Crosshill in 2020 — and her vision is still evolving, guided by her interest in history and observations of the site. She takes time to be in the garden, to notice what is growing where, and to plan from there. Nic is always on hand — often with his tractor, 'Blue' — prepared to drop whatever he's doing to help Ali realise her vision. They have banned sprays and replaced much of the grass with productive plants to feed the soil and their family.

The original double-gabled homestead was built around 1910. A century on, deteriorated beyond repair, it was provided to the local fire brigade to be burnt to the ground in a training exercise. At the same time the surrounding gardens were largely cleared, with the exception of a rose garden at the front of the house and the magnificent mature trees planted by the home's first owners. The native beech, copper beech, elderberry and liquidambar, as well as heritage plums, apples and cherries, survived to provide a sense of grandeur and structure for Ali's new vision for Crosshill. She suspects the rose garden was planted around the same time as the trees, and its original paved walkway connects her to these gardeners of long ago.

Kānuka and mānuka dotting the old sheep paddocks hint at what grew here before the land was cleared for agriculture. In the late nineteenth century the Crown agreed to restore the land rights to Ngāi Tahu, but the legislation was revoked in 1909 and the area was divided up for colonial agricultural settlement. Named after Kati Hāwea, one of the earliest tribes to occupy the South Island, Lake Hāwea supported seasonal food resources for Māori, with numerous kāinga mahinga kai (food-gathering places) and kāinga nōhoanga (settlements) established around the lake. Edible plants included kāuru (cabbage tree root), aruhe (bracken fernroot), and māra (gardens) of potato and turnip.

The hot, dry Central Otago summers facilitate a vegetable-growing season that is short, sharp and productive. Ever-passionate about growing food, Ali's vegetable garden and adjacent propagation and potting shed are central to Crosshill. She grows what she and Nic like to eat — brassicas, peas, cavolo nero (which grows exceptionally well), silverbeet, potatoes, leeks and carrots. The vegetable beds are fed with Ali's own compost, and dotted around the garden are small fencing-wire bins for collecting weeds as she works. These self-compost in situ and the contents are returned to the soil over time.

The property's varied terrain contributes to the contrasting environments — dry, wet, sun-drenched, cool — leading to a wide variety of planting opportunities, and sometimes new discoveries. One of these has been xeriscaping, a method of dry landscaping developed in Denver, Colorado, in response to increasing droughts.

The premise is to design plantings that require little or no watering. Ali has been researching extensively — and mulching heavily! Like all new methods, it's a process of trial and error, she says. She is looking at xeriscaping with both natives and exotics, and has realised that a lot of plants already in her garden, once well established and mulched, support her xeriscaping model.

The original orchard is being transformed into a five-layer permaculture food forest, its clipped lawns and sprayed edges replaced by luscious underplantings of comfrey, garlic chives, peas, lemon balm and other herbs. The deep taproot of comfrey brings up nutrients from the soil and makes them more accessible to the fruit trees, and its leaves are harvested for compost and for laying underneath potatoes when planting. Ali is planning to add grapevines, which will ramble through the branches of the existing fruit trees — apples, pears, apricots, peaches, feijoas and a much-loved quince.

The previous owners of Crosshill were passionate, talented gardeners but health issues meant that when Ali arrived some areas had been let go. The woodland area was barely accessible, with branches having been cut and left in situ. This did mean, however, that when Ali brought in a chipper and cleared the tangle of branches, she found rich, fertile soil underneath, fed by the decaying timber. The resulting chip was laid in the woodland, and the routes Ali's dogs took through the trees dictated the location of new paths.

Excavating a contained patch of Spanish bluebells, Ali discovered a deep trench of bulbs packed shoulder to shoulder. After careful lifting, dividing and replanting, these bluebells now line the woodland paths. In a clearing, a table enclosed in a halo of rhododendrons serves as a venue for family get-togethers and garden parties.

The many gardens of Crosshill are connected by the mature trees that form its bones, and Ali's overarching meditative gardening approach. The garden is a space for careful observation of all the elements that contribute to its magic — the seasons, soil conditions, wind direction, orientation of the sun and, most importantly, what likes to grow where. The constant conversation between garden and gardener is how each part of Ali's garden comes alive.

NOTES FROM ALI

WHAT IS XERISCAPING?

Xeriscaping is the technical term for dry landscaping, the art of choosing the right plants for a dry environment. Usually they are plants that require little to no water, other than what the natural climate in the area provides.

The term xeriscaping was coined in the early 1980s by the Denver Water Department, in response to a prolonged drought in the region. Residents of Denver were asked to conserve drinking water and reduce the watering of gardens and lawns.

Dry landscaping had been a recognised gardening style for many decades before that. At East Lambrook Manor Gardens in Somerset, plantswoman Margery Fish (1892–1969) dedicated a large area to drought-loving plants. Derek Jarman's garden at Dungeness in Kent survives beautifully in the shingle shore. Influential 'naturalistic' gardeners such as Piet Oudolf, Beth Chatto and Olivier Filippi have encouraged gardeners to look closely at the importance of sustainability within garden design.

Closer to home, Jo Wakelin has developed an outstanding garden on her dry gravel property on the banks of Lake Dunstan near Cromwell. Jo's garden is featured in the book *Wild: The Naturalistic Garden*, by Noel Kingsbury and Claire Takacs.

Simple tips for a dry landscape garden
'Right plant, right place' is my mantra when planning a garden. The starting point is to understand your landscape. All gardens have their own special requirements.

Cost is also a factor, so we want to ensure our plants will thrive where they are planted. Make sure you seek out drought-tolerant plants (or drought-loving plants, as I prefer to call them) when you are in the planning stage. Pay particular attention to plants that are native to your region. Silver, furry-leaf plants are naturally more drought tolerant.

Dry landscaping will be more successful if you follow these planting tips:

- Autumn is a good time to plant, as the natural rainfall of the cooler months will help the plants establish before the more demanding warmer weather arrives.
- Before planting, soak the plant in a bucket of water and seaweed tonic while you prepare the soil.
- Dig a hole twice the size of the root-ball. Add compost and water, allowing it to drain away before you plant.
- Plant to the same level as the plant sat in the pot. Some suggest agitating the roots a little to stimulate root growth.
- Fill the hole, water again, then mulch.

Mulch your xeriscaped garden with either bark chip or gravel to retain moisture before the ground heats up in summer and the soil dries out. Mulch will also help keep the weeds down. I prefer not to use weedmat/landscaping fabric because they are not biodegradable.

Irrigation systems are not required — that's the whole point. Hand-water with a hose if you have to, and if there are no restrictions in place. Reduce watering over time as the plants become established in their environment.

What to plant?

As I mentioned, you should research plants native to your environment, and take care to avoid (or keep an eye on) plants considered invasive.

Sempervivum (hen and chicks) succulents are a natural starting point for a dry garden. They are very useful along the edge of your border and in pots.

From there, the list is endless when you start to look! Here are some suggestions to get you started:

Native
Coprosma, griselinia, pseudopanax, phormium, cordyline, libertia, tussock grasses

Exotic
Lomandra, euphorbia, heuchera, hosta, agave, santolina, stipa

Bulbs
Daffodil, amaryllis, allium, nerine, scilla

Herbs
Rosemary, sage, oregano, thyme

For a touch of colour
Bearded iris, geranium, kangaroo paw, lavender, salvia, achillea, anemone, echinacea, cistus, phlomis, rudbeckia

Sustainable gardening, simply put, means gardening responsibly — in a way that preserves the natural environment, supports ecosystems, feeds the bees and nourishes your plants, all while causing no harm to the earth and its inhabitants, and enhancing your tūrangawaewae (place of standing).

+++

PROJECT: PUSSY WILLOW ARCH

The pussy willow trees in our garden (species unknown but probably *Salix cinerea*) had been cut down and allowed to regrow, a method called coppicing. (Coppicing takes the tree to ground level, while pollarding reduces the height of the tree to meet a specific requirement, for example stock fencing or privacy hedging.) The regrowth had been prolific and it was time to reduce the trees again, in order to reach the pussy willow blooms without using a fireman's ladder!

We liked the privacy afforded by the height of the trees, so we reduced the number of uprights by two-thirds instead of doing a complete coppice. The new regrowth would ensure enough low branches in spring to give us plenty of pussy willows for flower arrangements.

We set about our task in winter when the trees were dormant. We had intended to chip the branches to add to the compost heap, but they were quite beautiful in structure and I felt they had another purpose just waiting to become apparent. The branches were laid out on the grass — four of them about the same length, and all with two forks at approximately the same height.

Then it became obvious: the new purpose was an arbour. Not just any old arbour — this would be a living arbour. The four forked uprights formed the basic framework, to which we screwed horizontal branches cut to size. We then created the top of the arbour in a ladder shape.

The uprights were 'planted' in the ground approximately 40 centimetres deep. The top was secured in place with screws, and we added a kind of flying buttress support for stability. Then we waited. Spring was just around the corner and, full of hope, we watched as buds arrived on the uprights. It has been a delight to watch as the new growth appears each spring, though as yet we have only leaves, no catkins.

Other trees suitable for coppicing include hazelnut, chestnut, ash, eucalypts and elder. They are used for fencing and trellising, biomass, *hügelkultur* beds (raised garden beds filled with rotten wood), chop 'n' drop goodness for food forests, and firewood for efficient wood-burning systems. Personally, I use lots of coppiced material for making wreaths and plant support frames. We are fortunate in New Zealand — the amount of sunlight, our moisture levels and good soils mean that our tree growth is relatively fast compared with the UK.

+++

TEA GARDEN PLANTS

I love a cup of tea, and grow a large number of tea plants in my garden.

Leaves
Anise, lemon balm, lemon verbena, lemongrass, mint, tea bush (*Camellia sinensis*), holy basil, catmint, hyssop, nettle, passionflower, bronze fennel, rosemary, stevia, lemon thyme

Flowers
Anise hyssop, calendula, chamomile (German), cornflower, bergamot, lavender (English), red clover, hibiscus, sweet violet, pennyroyal, linden (tree), jasmine, rose, honeysuckle, saffron, yarrow

Fruits and seeds
Blackcurrant, blueberry, elderberry, goji berry, lemon, raspberry (leaves and berries), strawberry, rosehip, coriander, fenugreek, dill, fennel

Roots
Chicory, echinacea, ginger, licorice, turmeric, valerian, dandelion, purple angelica

A few of my favourite blends
Any of these tea blends can be sweetened with honey if desired.

- My go-to: Lemon, ginger and rosemary.
- Immune boosting: Mint, calendula, fennel seed and ginger.
- Digestive: Mint, chamomile, fennel seed and holy basil.
- Spring immunity and allergy relief: Fresh elderflowers — that's it! (Add lemon juice and honey if you like.)
- Winter immunity: Elderberries and cinnamon stick. Or spice it up for a real winter warmer with ginger, turmeric, lemon or orange juice.
- Raspberry leaf: 1 teaspoon dried raspberry leaf per cup of hot water. Delicious served cold with ice and a few raspberries added.

+ + +

A WAKE-UP CALL FOR GARDENERS

In the days before I was aware that bagged, peat-based potting mix was unethical, I purchased a bag to repot a few plants. The day was hot, I was frazzled and rushed and had no sharp implements to hand, so in my haste I bent over the bag and split it open with my teeth.

Fast forward four days and this normally very healthy individual was suffering with a severe fever and couldn't get out of bed. My doctor concurred that it was probably the flu but she requested a blood test and sent me home to bed. Less than two hours later I was in an ambulance on the way to hospital, after the CRP result showed a massive inflammatory reading.

Many tests and eight specialists later, a friend who is also a doctor took a look at my hospital records. She asked a question that had not been considered by the other professionals. 'Have you been using potting mix?' She knows me well. By this stage I was very sick. Double pneumonia had almost completely filled my lungs; my CRP count had reached the pre-mortem warning stage. '*Yes!*' I coughed. Immediate action was taken to treat me for Legionnaires' Disease, and that diagnosis saved my life. Many months of rest and recovery followed. My lungs are scarred, which restricts my activities, *but* I am alive, thanks to my friend's quick thinking.

My mission each spring over the past 10 years, since the silly decision that started it all, has been to educate people to *wear a mask and gloves when using bagged potting mix*. (And don't open the bags with your teeth...)

Legionella bacteria thrive and multiply in warm, moist conditions such as a plastic bag left in the sun. And of course your lungs are a perfect incubator.

Stay safe, lovely gardeners. If you have to use bagged potting mix, *please* wear a mask and gloves. And if you get flu-like symptoms, tell your doctor you have been using potting mix.

HAKEA

On a hillside in rural Raglan, overlooking Aotea Harbour and surrounded by Pakoka Scenic Reserve, is Hakea — a magical, off-grid, permaculture ecosystem designed to nourish mind, body and soul.

A family retreat since the 1990s, Hakea is more than a garden: it's a community and a way of living that is deeply connected to whenua. Hakea's gardeners observe and respond to their environment, nourishing the land, themselves and their community. WWOOFers (Worldwide Opportunities on Organic Farms), interns and sundry other garden helpers live in a few huts and old cottages dotted around the property.

The main garden on the 16-hectare property is a flat area that cuts into the sheltered north side of the hill. With its rich volcanic soil, it enjoys a subtropical climate, and shelter from protected native bush.

[W]e are on the cusp of a whole new world of learning around the life of soils and the relationship between our health and the soil our food is grown in . . . I think we need to be open-minded about how we can support and grow the soil so that it in turn can support and grow us . . . back into the interconnected web of life that we have been avoiding/ ignoring/ destroying for the last few generations!

— KAY BAXTER, *KOANGA GARDEN GUIDE*

ABOUT THE GARDENER

Hakea's head gardener is Turkish-born Merve (pronounced Mar-veh). While researching Drosophila fruit fly genetics on a cell biology internship in Scotland, Merve met Dan. He shared stories of New Zealand and his dream to live a self-sufficient life on a piece of land his parents had owned since the 1990s.

Merve grew up in a small remote village in the Black Sea region of northern Turkey. She had heard of New Zealand, but that was the extent of her knowledge. Her village is on a plateau surrounded by mountains, almost an hour away from the nearest town, Trabzon, and 30 minutes from the coast. To hear Merve talk about her early life is to be transported back to another time, when daily life was based around community, subsistence farming, resourcefulness and a deep connection to nature's seasonal rhythms.

The village economy centred on the cultivation of a few specialist crops, primarily hazelnuts and sweetcorn. Many of the resources in the village were shared; for example, one water tank served the whole community, and everyone shared responsibility for its maintenance. Farm machinery was scarce so a time-bank system provided extra labour when it was needed.

Apart from a few staples, such as olive oil, all food was grown in people's gardens or on the margins of their farmland — even the flour they used was made from their own corn. The villagers kept animals for meat, eggs and dairy products, making their own cheese, butter and yoghurt. Merve has no memory of buying fruit from a shop — she would just go into the forest with the other children, collecting whatever was in season.

As idyllic as life sounds, the weather high up in the mountains was extreme. In summer it would typically rain 20 days out of 30, giving the

village an almost tropical feel. By stark contrast, winter brought heavy snow from November to March. Crops nurtured through the short summer growing season were harvested and preserved in autumn to sustain the community through winter. Pickled vegetables were an important part of their winter diet, as were foraged nuts, berries and other fruit, preserved or frozen.

After the crops were harvested, all the women in the village pitched in to preserve the produce. In fact Merve's early memories are almost exclusively of women. Job opportunities in the village were scarce, so nearly all the men worked abroad, mainly in the building industry — including Merve's dad, whom she didn't meet until she was 11.

It was the women who kept the village going — running the farms, raising the children, helping out in one another's gardens. Looking back now, Merve realises that many of the gardening skills, cooperative systems and subsistence values our society is now trying to recreate were at work in her village, and had been for hundreds of years.

Merve was 11 when her family moved to Bursa, a large city close to Istanbul — for her father's work and in the hope of better educational opportunities for Merve and her siblings. She worked her way into the top 1 per cent for her university entrance exam and was selected to study sciences at one of the best universities in Turkey. All the courses were taught in English, so Merve's first year was an intensive English course, followed by four years of studying a wide spectrum of science subjects, from physics to biochemistry and biology.

A degree in molecular biology and genetics led her to work in research teams all around Europe, including Germany, Sweden and Scotland. She was particularly focused on cell biology. We all know that when you eat something it gets absorbed into your body, but Merve was concerned with what happens at a molecular level, such as how the chemicals bind to your genes, and where the protein goes. Her commitment to permaculture is informed by her scientific knowledge, and fed by a compulsion to constantly research and learn about gardening processes.

Her transition to life in rural Raglan was not easy, however. Although the setting was idyllic, Merve had trouble finding a job in science, couldn't drive and didn't know anyone. After the vibrancy of European cities, she struggled to adjust to the isolation of Hakea. In those early days she had little interest in gardening, and 'zero' gardening knowledge. Then, in 2017, Dan acquired some heritage tomato seeds — and their growth caught

Merve's interest. These first seeds lit the spark that would go on to create Hakea as it is today.

Merve eventually found a job as an air-quality technician at Hill Laboratories in Hamilton, mainly working in analytical chemistry. Meanwhile, in her downtime the vegetable garden gradually expanded, in what she describes now, looking back, as a somewhat haphazard way. As her interest — and their harvests — grew, Merve became aware of a local 'crop swap'. She joined up and it was here that she met Claire, who was to become her gardening mentor. For the next few months Merve went to Claire's garden for a few hours each week to help out, along the way learning about soil health, making hot compost, crop rotation, companion planting, making potting mix and propagating plants from seed and from cuttings.

A few years after arriving at Hakea with Dan, Merve obtained a scholarship to study permaculture design at Tui Community in Golden Bay, where she discovered that permaculture was more about community than growing things. Next she completed a Kai Oranga (food sustainability) course through Te Whare Wānanga o Awanuiārangi, where she learned a huge amount about Māori culture and the way Māori relate to the land. During walks in the bush she learnt about rongoā (medicines), about tikanga (customs), how to harvest plants and how to treat them with respect. It made Merve aware of the spiritual context that she felt had been missing from permaculture teachings. She came to understand that there is a wairua, a spirit, in the land, and the gardener is part of that. The garden and the gardener are not distinct from each other — they are connected.

The Kai Oranga course also reconnected Merve to her own whakapapa — the village she grew up in, the community that lived according to the rhythms of nature. It was at this point that everything came together — her upbringing in Turkey, her science degree and research, her permaculture knowledge, the Hakea whenua and local indigenous knowledge. The course finished in June 2021, and Merve quit her job at the end of July to work full time in the gardens at Hakea, as head gardener, permaculture designer and educator.

ABOUT THE GARDEN

Hakea has two main gardens: a forest garden and a vegetable garden. Both are sustained by compost, chickens, recycled rainwater, and the Hakea residents' commitment to whenua and community.

The main garden (now the forest garden) was established by Dan's parents and used intermittently over the years. It occupies a flat area that is a bit of a frost pocket. Morning sun is blocked by a big olive tree and some natives, so the garden gets most of its sun in the afternoon.

Merve extended this garden with some help, and called it the forest garden because of its diverse array of plants — fruit trees, perennials, annuals, herbs, medicinal plants and carbon-fixing crops. It is a closed-loop ecosystem of plants nourishing and supporting one another, meaning gardener intervention is minimal. Dense planting controls weeds and promotes soil moisture retention. Merve mulches as much as she can and plants lots of seedlings, and the rest of her time in this garden is spent observing, harvesting and enjoying it.

A forest garden starts with a tree and works outwards from there. Alongside the fruit trees are carbon crops, which are grown to chop 'n' drop. This includes anything that has a stalk that withstands wind — sunflowers, Jerusalem artichokes, globe artichokes, wheat, corn, dogwood, comfrey and woody herbs such as lavender and rosemary. Cut down, these act like fallen leaves in a forest, creating biomass, encouraging fungal growth and breaking down to feed the soil. Next come berries, herbs, and flowering and medicinal plants.

The tendency of nature to regenerate as a forest — a diverse, self-supporting ecosystem — is Merve's model for this garden. By closely observing its growth, she is supporting this ecosystem rather than forcing it in any predetermined direction. The forest garden is wild — Merve describes her personal gardening style as 'quite chaotic' — and utterly magical. Beans winding up blackberry bushes create peaceful hidden grottos, with colours and textures at every level, a steady stream of insect traffic, and the chorus of birdlife in the surrounding native bush.

For all that is happening *in* the forest garden, just as much is happening beneath it. Merve's approach to soil health is deeply influenced by Kay Baxter of Kōanga. Nutrient-dense and microbially active soil grows nutrient-dense food. Broccoli grown in healthy, carbon-dense soil full of microbes will have many more nutrients than broccoli grown with synthetic fertilisers.

The vegetable garden, or 'hot garden', is a more recent addition. Built into the side of a north-facing slope, it gets all-day sun, easterly winds and no frost, providing a sheltered micro-climate for growing herbs and vegetables all year round. Terraced gardens protrude from a steep slope overlooking the valley of dense native bush. Aside from asparagus and pineapple, everything grown here is edible annuals and pollinators. It is densely planted with an exceptionally diverse number of species, planted in clumps and layers rather than straight rows. The effect is colourful, lush and textured.

Possums have been a huge challenge at Hakea. When Merve first arrived they were rampant, eating everything in the garden. It felt like a battle the humans could never win. However, with the help of WWOOFers they embarked on the gargantuan project of building a corrugated-iron fence right around the gardens. Using recycled or donated materials, and with an electric wire around the top, the fence has made all the difference. The possum situation in the bush generally, though, remains serious. The damage these introduced mammals cause to native bush and bird populations is devastating, and Merve supports Te Iwi Tahi o Karioi, a hapū-led group that works to control the possum population in the district.

With their possum-proof fence, wider Hakea community and deep commitment to regenerating healthy, productive ecosystems, Merve and Dan are well on their way to achieving their vision for Hakea. For Merve, the colourful, diverse and somewhat unruly gardens she has created are an expression of herself through nature. They are the tangible manifestation of the connectedness of everything.

NOTES FROM MERVE

BUILDING YOUR SOIL

To grow strong, healthy plants you need healthy soil. Your soil and all it contains — worms, microbes, fungi — need constant nourishment. I cannot stress this enough. Microbes in our soil web unlock the minerals and make these available to our plants, which then are able to grow healthy and disease/pest free.

For me there are four key 'pillars' to soil health — composting, growing carbon crops, crop rotation and mulching.

Everything starts with the soil: the success of your gardening depends on it.

Composting

Making great compost ensures that the garden gets high-quality carbon and minerals. The goal of composting is to create humus that carries a living biological form of carbon and minerals to feed the soil microbes. This part of the soil will also hold on to water, meaning less time spent watering. Pests and diseases will be reduced and the plants will be able to grow to their maximum potential in nutrient density.

Building a compost pile is like making lasagne. The pile has roughly equal amounts of two essential components — carbon inputs and nitrogen inputs. The carbon layer is brown: think autumn leaves, corn stems, sunflower stalks, grain stalks, artichoke stalks. The nitrogen layer is green: weeds, kitchen waste, manure, comfrey and grass clippings.

To make the best compost we need to use as many different materials as possible to enrich the nutrient mix. Start the pile with rough material such as twigs, small branches and stalks, to help aerate the pile as it grows. Then add a carbon layer, followed by a green layer. The next layer is soil, to make sure minerals are held in the heap and microbes are happy. Include as many mineral sources as you can find — such as burnt bones, lime, seaweed.

Water each layer as you go. When you take a handful of compost material and squeeze it, you should get a drop or two of water coming out. If it's soggier than that you'll end up with anaerobic compost.

Don't compact it down too much. Loosen it up with a fork every so often to ensure the pile is aerated.

Growing carbon crops

Carbon is nature's building block — it's the element that connects other elements together, giving soil the ability to hold nutrients. Half of our garden is planted in carbon-accumulator crops such as corn, grains, sunflowers, Jerusalem artichokes and globe artichokes. These and other plants with tough stems contain a material called lignin, which decomposes into complex structures that protect and store carbon, nitrogen and other minerals. Growing your own carbon crops ensures you will always have enough carbon to make enough compost to feed your soil.

Crop rotation

Crop rotation is an important part of keeping the soil healthy and balanced while growing nutrient-dense food. Different plants have different nutrient needs, so you want to avoid growing the same crop in the same place year after year, or you will exhaust the soil's supply of the nutrients that particular crop needs. Your rotation should be a minimum of three years.

There are many approaches to crop rotation. I like to follow the cycle of leaf and fruit (heavy feeders), followed by roots and legumes, and lastly carbon crops.

HEAVY FEEDERS: These can be divided into two groups, leaf and fruit. Leaf plants include brassicas, lettuce, spinach and kale, all of which have high nitrogen needs. Fruit plants include tomatoes, squash, peppers and pumpkin, which need phosphorus.

ROOTS AND LEGUMES: Root vegetables include leeks, beets, radishes and carrots, which need potassium. Legumes include peas, beans and lupins, which fix nitrogen in the soil.

CARBON CROPS: These include corn, sunflowers, grains and lupins.

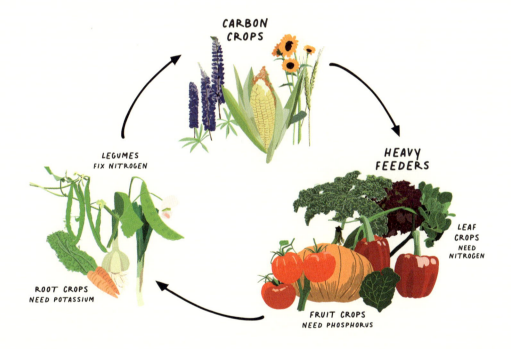

Mulching

Adding a generous layer of mulch to your garden mimics the natural process that takes place in nature, and provides so many benefits — aiding moisture retention, providing nutrients and organic matter for your soil,

and suppressing weed growth. It also helps to regulate soil temperature, and provides the perfect conditions for beneficial fungi to thrive.

You can use pea straw, 'chop and drop' non-seedling weeds, trimmings or prunings, or use a chipper to make your own nutrient-dense ramial wood chips — wood chips made from smaller, freshly cut branches (typically up to 7-centimetre diameter), that are still 'green', with or without their leaves.

+ + +

DESIGNING A FOREST GARDEN

A forest garden is a diverse and integrated system that consists of a variety of trees, bushes, shrubs, herbs, vines and groundcovers. High density and diversity — through many layers above ground and many layers of roots below ground — will create a 'wilder' system that will be healthier, happier and require less maintenance.

The idea is to create a closed nutrient cycle whereby all the nutrients and minerals that are important for growth are collected by microorganisms in the soil web and taken up by the plants' roots. The plants utilise these nutrients during photosynthesis, and at the end of the cycle the leaves return to the soil, for those nutrients to be recaptured by the soil web. This closed nutrient cycle, keeping valuable nutrients and minerals in the system, means we don't have to bring nutrients in (fertiliser, compost).

The key is to plant your forest garden in layers, to mimic the stacking found in tropical rainforests, where plants are layered to share light, water and nutrients. The seven layers of a forest garden are:

- canopy trees
- low tree layer
- shrubs
- herbaceous layer of perennials (chop 'n' drop)
- groundcover
- root crops
- vines or vertical layer.

Forest ecology incorporates three key types of plants to stabilise and build the soil in preparation for creating a forest with many layers. These are:

BIOMASS PRODUCERS: Plants that grow fast and are useful to chop 'n' drop — tagasaste or tree lucerne, sunflowers, eucalypts, artichokes and comfrey.

NITROGEN FIXERS: Plants that fix nitrogen in the soil — tagasaste or tree lucerne, tree lupin (*Lupinus arboreus*), locust trees (*Gleditsia triacanthos*), clover, lupins and any sort of beans.

MINERAL ACCUMULATORS: Plants that mine nutrients and minerals, releasing them to the soil so other plants can use them. Many herbs and flowers do this, including comfrey, borage, chicory, daikon radish, amaranth, mulberry and nettles (avoiding the highly poisonous *Urtica ferox*!).

+ + +

GROWING MEDICINE

A forest system provides medicine for its occupants. For example, if a forest animal was sick, it would instinctively find the right herb to eat and heal. From the same perspective, we are a part of the forest garden we designed, therefore including the element of medicine is vital.

Herbal remedies are medicines made from homegrown or foraged plants that are used to help prevent or cure medical problems. There are dozens of herbs and plants that can be used for this purpose. We currently grow lavender, rosemary, thyme, raspberry leaf, chamomile, lemon balm, mint, peppermint, dandelion, clover, feverfew, yarrow, plantain, selfheal, calendula, kawakawa, angi angi, comfrey, valerian, ashwagandha, elecampane and marshmallow.

We use these herbs to make tea, tinctures, infused oils and healing balms.

+ + +

MARAMATAKA

Maramataka is the traditional Māori lunar calendar, which can be used in all sorts of decision-making and management processes. One of its functions was to guide the gathering of kai, including gardening and fishing. Gardening by the moon has been practised for many centuries. The strong gravitational pull of the moon affects the moisture levels in soil, as well as how quickly seeds germinate and plants grow.

Maramataka is derived from the word marama, meaning the moon. Thus, Maramataka uses stars and lunar phases.

Whiro (new moon)
As the moon grows, light and gravitational pull start to increase. Seeds sown during this period have a high chance of germinating. Strong sap flow encourages plants to grow, so this is a good time for transplanting and to start fertilising. Whiro is the night of the new moon.

First quarter
This is a productive time in the garden, ideal for sowing or transplanting fruiting and flowering crops. The light becomes stronger while the pull becomes less. This makes it a good time for leaf crops. With the sap flowing, there is a lot of growth above ground.

Rākaunui (full moon)
There is high energy three days before and three days after the full moon. This is a good time for fertilising, but seed sowing and transplanting should be avoided. High energy will cause a flush of growth followed by weak plants.

Last quarter
After the full moon, sap starts flowing downwards, supporting strong and healthy roots. This is a good time to sow root crops, and for transplanting. The time of rest comes as the light and gravitational pull decreases. This is a good time to prune, harvest and weed the garden.

VIOLET'S GARDEN

On a hilltop in suburban Dunedin is Violet's Garden, an ever-evolving collage of botanical curiosities, foraged weeds and rare flowering perennials.

In the 10 years she has gardened here, Violet has created numerous gardens, including a woodland area, a planted berm, vegetable patches, a bog garden and a shade garden. Each is distinct but exists in considered connection to its neighbours.

Violet describes her gardening influences as a materials-led mixtape of textures, colours and feelings: the warm bright flowers set against a dark background on her childhood eiderdown quilt, the Sussex woodland countryside painted in blocks of colour by Ivon Hitchens from his home caravan, Victorian block-printed wallpapers, summer horse rides through dusty tracks of yarrow and cow parsley.

It is just in the way it is done that lies the whole difference between commonplace gardening and gardening that may rightly claim to rank as a fine art . . . [plants] may be fashioned into a dream of beauty, a place of perfect rest and refreshment of mind and body — a series of soul-satisfying pictures — a treasure of well-set jewels . . .

— GERTRUDE JEKYLL, *COLOUR IN THE FLOWER GARDEN*

ABOUT THE GARDENER

Gardening has been the constant in Violet's life. She grew up on the rural outskirts of Timaru, one of four children to doctor parents. On a big property surrounding an old farmhouse, the garden of Violet's childhood was rambling and tangled. Her mother, Gladys, spent what time she could in the garden, growing vegetables and creating a flower garden reminiscent of the English cottage gardens of her own childhood. Mother and daughter worked in the garden together and, although Violet's colour palette today is markedly different, the beautiful, wild garden of her childhood has hugely influenced the way she gardens today.

Violet remembers a lake surrounded by wild dog roses on a family holiday in Alexandra, ice plants tumbling down ocean cliffsides, and lupins growing out of the dry riverbeds of the Mackenzie Country (some of which she now knows to be 'beautiful pollution'). The sensations of magic in these wild accidental gardens still drive her gardening practice. Weekends were spent outdoors, and Gladys trusted her young daughter in the garden, inviting her to contribute to design decisions and even help build a pond. There was no paid help; they did everything themselves, repurposing discarded farm machinery and laying their own bricks for little seated areas and paths.

At around age seven, Violet secretly planted a garden of moss and primroses in her bedroom. She watered it diligently until, the carpet beneath having rotted, water seeped through the floor, dripping into the kitchen below. Her secret was out.

In 2019 Violet gave up her vintage clothing store in Dunedin and began working full time as a gardener and garden designer, dividing her

time between her own garden and those of a few select clients. Her shop specialised in pre-1950s clothing and natural fabrics. She had worked on costumes in the film industry and this affection for fashion was another iteration of Violet's material-driven creative practice. Before opening the vintage store she was an exhibiting visual artist. Actual plants often featured in her work — gallerists had to remember to 'water the art' daily.

Violet also sang in a band. Space Dust, formed in Ōtautahi Christchurch in 1993, described themselves as 'seldom surfacing for more than a single gig every couple of years'. Although she doesn't draw specific connections between her gardening, fashion, artwork and music, perhaps the connections are inherent in the very nature of creative practices. Gardening is performative even in the most secret of gardens: the gardener at work, and the plants constantly transforming. The performance of gardening is a collaboration, too, between the plants, the seasons, the insect and bird life and the soil biota. The intermittent performances of Space Dust perhaps echoed the stubborn recurrence of Violet's perennials.

In a Christchurch flat years ago, Violet took down a fence and merged gardens with the botanist who lived next door. They made a pond and, having carried scavenged windows home one at a time on her bicycle, Violet built an octagonal glasshouse. Found materials also featured in her art, too, many of them installations involving an element of sound. *Be Kind* (1996), a video work that exposed a gardener's internal monologue, was made in this garden.

In a 2001 exhibition catalogue essay, curator Tessa Laird called Violet's use of found objects 'a charitable act of resuscitation, nevertheless feel[ing] no pity for the objects that she salvages; pity implies abjection'. A similar detachment informs her attitude towards her plants. 'If a plant in your garden isn't pleasing you in its appearance or positioning, get rid of it. Give it away! There are too many exciting plants in the world to continually be considering/evaluating the merits of one that's bugging you.'

There are many gardens Violet loves, but they're not *her* garden. They're not her wombled-together, magical garden on the hill above Dunedin, surrounding a Victorian cottage that in winter is draped in snow. Among the gardening styles she admires are those of contemporary landscape gardener Dan Pearson, who specialises in naturalistic perennials; and Gertrude Jekyll (1843–1932), who spearheaded the Arts and Crafts movement alongside architect Edwin Lutyens, intricately documenting her informal gardening methods through writing and photography.

Also on Violet's list is landscape designer Alasdair Cameron's garden in Devon, with its soft wildness of grasses and late summer perennials. She recently enjoyed reading the correspondence between British gardeners Christopher Lloyd and Beth Chatto, published in 2021 as *Dear Friend and Gardener: Letters on Life and Gardening*. Violet was interested that their friendship as gardeners thrives despite, or perhaps in part because of, their contrasting approaches to gardening.

ABOUT THE GARDEN

When Violet and her husband Malcolm bought their Dunedin house in 2012 their daughters Clara and Emerald were still young, so Violet prioritised getting a vegetable garden started. The house was grey with a grey roof, net curtains, a square rose garden with a few neglected inhabitants, some overgrown shrubs, and a straggly pittosporum hedge separating the property from the street. But the section was bigger than any she'd had before, and Violet knew that this would be her 'forever garden'. She could see past the bark chip layered over black polythene, and relished the idea of releasing its potential.

With the vegetable patch started, out came the pittosporum hedge and in went the main border, now the sunniest, most abundant garden. Most of the shrubs came out too, retaining just a smoke bush and a pollarded maple, and that area is now a woodland garden. Where black polythene once dominated is now the shady border or 'spooky bed'.

During Covid-19 lockdowns a pond was dug to replace the rose garden. Most of the roses were past it, and besides, Violet could never make sense of roses being planted all together just because they're roses.

Aside from a little glasshouse, the back garden was bare lawn. The neighbour's discarded glasshouse has now been connected to the existing one, and Violet dug out the floor space to lay down a terracotta tiled floor. She now has a nursery area where she raises plants for her own garden and to sell from a street-side stall. The vegetable beds and flower beds are slowly expanding into the lawn space, ever evolving. She has also planted the grass berm out front, so that the garden extends beyond the property, blurring the public–private space boundary and providing enjoyment for passers-by.

Most of the soil is heavy clay, with the exception of a few loamy patches that Violet supposes are vegetable patches from times gone by. She has been painstakingly breaking up the clay with compost and mulch. Her preferred mulch is pea straw — for its insulating qualities and the 'silkiness' it adds to the soil as it breaks down.

She doesn't introduce anything inorganic into the garden — just homemade compost and seaweed tonic, or a little neem oil spray. On the hill above Dunedin's greenbelt, the property is largely sheltered but the wind does whip through sometimes. Snowy winters and generally short mild summers mean everything Violet plants needs to be fairly hardy.

She doesn't tend to plan much, just the odd sketch that is seldom followed. Violet gardens intuitively, developing each little area as the mood takes her: a bog garden, a shade garden, a drought garden, a fancifully moory pond. Part of this is trying to have the right plant in the right place so that she's not wasting resources and water. She's always ready to move a plant if it is not thriving, or looks out of place.

Perennials are Violet's specialisation. Often considered more challenging to grow and with less instant reward than annuals, perennials grow, seed and die, then repeat this process the following year. Grasses that are not officially ornamental — oats, rye, barley — grow among her perennials for extra texture, as well as 'weeds' such as wild parsnip and thistle. Teasel seeds (*Dipsacus fullonum*) have been harvested from a Central Otago roadside, and wild black mullein (*Verbascum nigrum*) from a riverbank.

In winter she allows her plants to seed and die right down, opting to support their natural processes rather than 'tidy up'. She enjoys their twiggy stems and the dewy spiderwebs glittering in the frost.

Violet always has a list of plants she's looking for that are hard to find. Recently she collaborated with her gardener friend Susie Ripley to import a collection of perennial seeds. Susie runs a garden shop and online retail business, so she managed the importing logistics, and together they sourced 40 perennial varieties they had not been able to find in Aotearoa. They included plume poppy (*Macleaya microcarpa*), with large flat intricately geometric leaves and puffy white flower plumes, and Korean bellflower (*Campanula takesimana*), with a dusty pink canopy of hanging bell-shaped blooms. Violet painted botanical illustrations for the seed packets that might be equally appropriate for a witchcraft pharmacology manual or a Dries Van Noten runway textile.

Gardens are self-portraits. Violet always works alone on hers. It's indulgent and creative and there's not really space for others' input. Her open-garden events are a way to share the joy, though, and she's known among friends for always being late to dinner parties, but always arriving with an armful of flowers.

Violet hopes her self-portrait is a little eccentric and idiosyncratic, with its foraged weeds and palette of ox blood, biscuity browns and butter. She sees gardeners as being like musicians or readers: diverse and deeply personal in their tastes and fixations.

If she were to offer any advice to other gardeners, it would be to make bold choices, and to trust themselves.

NOTES FROM VIOLET

BUILDING A POND

My fascination with water in a garden goes way back.

Tiny me couldn't keep away from water and found the water lillies in the Timaru Botanic Gardens pond completely magical and exotic. I wanted to take a piece home — a compulsion I often have when looking at beautiful gardens and landscapes. My pockets are well used and grubby with the seed heads, blooms or what Mum called 'heels' that have made their way in there.

I dream (literally and figuratively) of having water in my garden deep enough to bathe in. I made my first permanent pond for my mother around age 16. It was concrete and I decorated it with vintage ceramic pieces. A wishing well came soon after — a small, deep sculpted concrete basin sunk into one of Mum's rock gardens.

When flatting in Christchurch I made another small pond/bog garden. From memory it was unlined and constantly drained . . . There were also two cast-iron baths with claw feet outdoors — one with lilies and fish and the other a fire bath (a bathtub with a fire under it to heat the water) for humans.

In our first home I built a small pond in the courtyard, with broken Edwardian china mosaics decorating the lip. The wee ones would play in it.

Concrete ponds are sometimes problematic because tree roots can disrupt them and compromise the structural integrity. I was always patching leaks and cracks in the one I made for Mum. My dream is for a natural pond, but that's not something I've achieved yet. I need to find the time to do more research.

My current pond was dug during a Covid lockdown. I used the least useful part of the garden in terms of growing — a dry, low-lit area with tree roots and rock-hard clay soil. It's also a sloped area, so I used the soil I dug out to build up a bank with a flattened top. (This was supposed to be used for seating and a fire pit, but somehow it ended up planted in perennials!)

I draped a hose to 'draw' a shape that felt natural within the space. Then I dug it with a spade. All was going well until I struck a drainpipe with my spade and broke it. Luckily it was an easy fix, with a water-resistant adhesive sealant. By this stage Malcolm was looking on nervously. This is not uncommon; he knows my projects are often driven by an urgency to complete what's in my mind's eye, often with little or no practical knowledge . . .

The pond dug, I sourced a decent-quality, UV-resistant plastic liner. A bit cheap and nasty but I didn't want to use concrete in an area so full of tree roots.

I got a little advice and reassurance from my friend Elizabeth. She is in her seventies and I'm in awe of her gardens, as well as her pond-making and building skills. Elizabeth used a digger to create huge farm ponds using polythene liners, so if they were good enough for her I was sold.

The process was simple. Before laying the plastic liner I bedded the dug-out area with sand to protect the liner from any sharp objects. (I was advised against using old carpet as it often has tacks hiding in it.)

Then I laid the plastic on the sand, leaving an allowance of a good 30 centimetres around the edge, and started to fill it with water. This is best done on a warmer day when the plastic is more malleable. As you fill, you can manipulate the polythene to get rid of creases. Once it was full and free of creases I trimmed the edges and disguised any visible liner with river stones and later plants.

The pond is home to several goldfish — no frogs as yet, but fingers crossed they will find it soon. I haven't installed a filter; instead I'm endeavouring to strike the perfect balance of pond plants to filter the water naturally — submerged (nitrogen fixers), floating (which protect the pond from the sun and therefore hamper algae growth) and marginal pond plants. Currently it still needs the occasional clean in the sunny months. I built in a wee drain hole and underground pipe that takes the dirty water to the driest area of my garden.

It's definitely a disadvantage that there is no naturally damp bog. Where a natural pond supports marginal plants, an artificial pond like mine goes straight from wet to dry — in my case to pretty awful heavy clay. To create the feeling of a more natural pond I dug an area around the edge and buried my left-over liner, punctured it roughly with a fork and filled it with rich compost. This is enough to retain some moisture and collect pond overflow in heavy rain. This edge is now home to many moisture-loving species:

umbrella plant (*Darmera peltata*), *Astilboides tabularis*, *Astilbe* spp., *Rodgersia* spp. and *Filipendula* spp.

I love that the pond can be dipped into during drought times for a bucket of water to toss on the garden — of course it collects any rainfall. I also love that it's a perfect system: the fish nibble plants and their waste breaks down to feed the plants.

It's certainly encouraging more wildlife — mainly cheeky blackbirds, dragonflies, may beetles, various water creatures I don't yet know the names of . . . and countless little people. It's a busy wee community.

WELLINGTON GARDEN

Jacob and Lucy's Stokes Valley garden is rarely quiet. Tūī and korimako (bellbirds) are regular noisy visitors from the mass of native bush that borders their property. Over the past couple of years the birds have witnessed the couple lugging many a bag of compost and bucket of seaweed into the garden to create their native nursery and organic supermarket.

It hasn't always been this way: just a few years earlier the garden had a decidedly untamed vibe, and was almost entirely shaded by overgrown exotic trees.

Since buying the Lower Hutt property in 2021, Jacob and Lucy have wasted no time rethinking and designing their site and putting their self-sufficiency plans into action. Two years on, the 3000 square-metre-section (three-quarters of an acre, much of it in 40-year-old native bush) is almost unrecognisable. Just 30 minutes out of central Wellington, the garden they are creating is an oasis for the couple and their sons, Archie, aged three, and Mack, 10 months.

Lucy and Jacob's original quest for food resilience didn't take long to transition into a greater, more pressing purpose — regenerating the native bush has become a self-described obsession. 'There are so many benefits to incorporating natives into your garden,' Jacob says. 'Even if your focus is vegetable growing, it's all connected — connected to soil health, the microbes and fungi in the soil. It's all about strengthening that complex web.'

At the beginning of the twenty-first century, the dreams of New Zealanders as a gardening people stand awaiting fulfilment. The importance of locally grown food will increase in the coming decades because the global food system is in need of a dramatic and inevitable shake-up.

— MATT MORRIS, *COMMON GROUND:
GARDEN HISTORIES OF AOTEAROA*

ABOUT THE GARDENERS

Lucy and Jacob both found their green fingers in their late twenties. Neither had much interest in gardening when they met at 19, studying at Victoria University, Wellington — Lucy an accounting major and Jacob a sociology major. But a strong connection to nature was present in both their childhoods.

Lucy grew up under North Canterbury's hills in Culverden on a crop and sheep farm. Her mother was, and still is, a passionate gardener, developing and maintaining an impressive English-style country garden set among mature specimen trees. Lucy remembers hydrangeas, roses and manicured box hedging, and topiary in the shape of cantering horses — a playful nod to the family's equestrian bent. It was an idyllic adventure playground for Lucy and her siblings, who would spend hours roaming the garden and playing on the flying foxes their dad strung through the garden — some well over 30 metres long.

Jacob grew up in Lake Ōkāreka, Rotorua, on a bush-clad section. His strongest garden memory though is of going to his godmother's home in West Auckland once a year. It was a real wonderland. He remembers picking beans off the vine, trees laden with fruit, his godmother Connie preserving everything. A young Jacob thought eating bottled fruit and ice-cream for lunch every day was magic.

His father got into gardening at some point when he was a bit older — he was a tomato and garlic man. There was a period when all the family would be given garlic knots for Christmas. After graduating from university, Jacob trained in the family business as a pounamu carver. On reflection, he says he has found a similar satisfaction in growing his own food —

gardening, like carving, is a craft requiring a methodical approach, refining your techniques as you go, taking pride in your work.

For a while Jacob lived in London, which was where he started to 'go deep' into food supply chains, learning about where food comes from. A new business called Farmdrop was competing with the big supermarket chains. People could order food to be delivered directly from local, sustainable food growers, completely cutting out the 'middle man', reducing food miles and sidestepping 'big agriculture' mass food producers.

Jacob thought it was a great idea and one that he could potentially bring back to New Zealand. In the event another company beat him to it, but his research had led him to the realisation that the current supermarket model was unsustainable on so many levels — food miles, damaging agricultural practices, loss of topsoil and biodiversity through mass production, and diminishing food resilience in communities that relied on this system. He realised that growing his own food was the ultimate way to shorten the supply chain.

The opportunity did not present itself until a few years later, when he and Lucy returned to New Zealand and were living temporarily with Jacob's parents in Wellington's Aro Valley. Through the gate in his parents' back fence was a large allotment-style community garden, and he and Lucy were instantly intrigued. Before long they had taken over a plot of their own. They began experimenting as complete beginners, planting an assortment of lettuces, cucumbers and tomatoes but without much success. That first year they got some average-tasting tomatoes and not much else.

They started watching other gardeners at work in the 50 community plots to see how they were doing it. 'It always felt quite voyeuristic,' Jacob says. 'When no one was there we'd walk around and look at everything, checking to see what was going on in people's polytunnels, what they were growing, what stage things were at, what looked healthy.'

If other gardeners were around they'd strike up conversations about what they were doing and why . . . and bit by bit their knowledge and confidence grew. A few years after their first growing foray they found their 1940s property in Stokes Valley, the large section ripe with potential.

Jacob and Lucy describe the previous owners as 'wild gardeners' — they took a *laissez-faire* approach to the garden, by and large leaving it to do its own thing. There was a lot of work to be done when they moved in, but Lucy and Jacob were up for the challenge. They now spend as much time as possible in the garden and bush, Archie and Mack at their feet (often their six chickens, too). The garden is all-consuming, but all giving — having become their shared hobby, gym substitute, holiday destination, greengrocer and intellectual pursuit.

Two years into their home-gardening journey, the pair have their sights set firmly on nurturing a sanctuary for native flora and fauna and a haven for their whanau.

ABOUT THE GARDEN

On what was once a shaded and neglected back lawn, Lucy and Jacob's vegetable garden now thrives. Spinach, rhubarb, spring onions and lettuces burst from the soil, bordered by bricks. Montbretia poke their orange heads towards potatoes and thick green leeks. Among the carrots and cauliflower, lancewood, miro, nīkau palms and putaputawētā have self-sown and established themselves. Young tōtara, black beech, tawa and juvenile rimu around the garden's perimeter extend leafy arms towards the veges — they'll be transplanted into the forest when they are ready.

'Think cottage garden meets native forest restoration,' says Jacob. 'Also think "work in progress"!' adds Lucy. The edible garden area is about 200 square metres, including the fruit trees. Feijoa trees and blueberry bushes bask in pockets of light. The property was originally farmland, and the previous owners planted up the property in the 1940s with large specimen trees and a few natives such as black beeches.

Jacob convinced Lucy that digging up the lawn would be their best option, and then set about formulating a planting plan. They started watching a lot of gardening content on YouTube and reading voraciously. Gardeners like Charles Dowding, Kay Baxter and Kath Irvine provided ample inspiration and advice that seemed impartial and science-driven. Jacob has no time for old wives' tales.

The garden took shape on paper, guided by research and careful observation of the site. Sunlight was scarce on their valley site, so they used a smartphone app to help them understand the course of the sun and observe how its arc changes throughout the year. Their northern boundary was a wall of massive well-established exotic trees and they decided around 10 of those needed to be cut down in order to increase their sun.

'The entire section pretty much lost sun by about 12.30 p.m., so it needed to happen. It was painful to cut down trees, especially a liquidambar whose leaves would turn blood red in autumn, but we got about two more hours of sun in the garden after that. Even so, most of the veges only get five or six hours of sun a day, which is classified as semi-shade. Full sun is six hours or more.'

They began by aerating the hard-packed clay soil with a broad fork (Jacob's new favourite garden implement), then laid down cardboard and dumped 9 cubic metres of compost from the Wellington City recycling facility on top. The addition of worm castings to the 'dead compost' helped bring the soil to life, the humus in the castings boosting the soil's water retention and aeration, anchoring nutrients that otherwise drip away with water.

The soil was further augmented with seaweed powder supplements from Seacliff Organics in Dunedin, which they also now use as a foliar spray directly onto their crops and fruit trees. Serious mulching with pea straw has also helped improve the quality of the soil, as well as retaining moisture and suppressing weeds.

There have been setbacks of course. Fruit trees were planted where sunlight didn't quite reach: a nectarine tree shrivelled up and died. There was a potato crop that suffered from potato scab, great brown spots spreading over their skin.

Jacob, a self-confessed digital nerd, has everything recorded on a spreadsheet now — when they plant, species names and how many seedlings they put in. This record-keeping and close analysis has helped them track their successes and failures and adjust their plan accordingly as they get to know the niche conditions of their valley site. Their garden planning is also strongly influenced by the lunar calendar, which they follow closely.

They quickly came to realise that local knowledge was like gold, and particularly latched on to Kath Irvine's Edible Backyard online resource (ediblebackyard.co.nz). Irvine was living up the coast in Ōhau, south of Levin. But no two sites, however close geographically, are identical, with different prevailing winds, soil types and daylight hours. Jacob and Lucy have had to adapt their own timings through trial and error.

After what Jacob had come to understand about the loss of biodiversity inherent in the 'big agriculture' model, deciding to only plant heritage

varieties was a no-brainer. Kōanga is their go-to for seed purchasing — they specialise in preserving and protecting older varieties of fruits and vegetables. 'They are delicious,' says Lucy. 'Unlike most of the vegetables you get from the supermarket, they actually have flavour! By growing heritage varieties, we are protecting the old strains and we feel like we are doing our little bit.'

Figuring out a rainwater irrigation system is the next job, with summer water restrictions becoming increasingly common. Growing heritage seedlings to supply the community is also on the cards. They have their eyes set on acquiring a glasshouse, having found that raising seedlings in the living room in the middle of winter has its drawbacks . . .

Their advice for other beginner gardeners? Find someone nearby who is producing the sorts of things you want to grow, and ask their advice. 'Being local, their recommendations are going to be super relevant and there's less chance of getting disheartened and giving up. That was partly our impetus for joining Secret Gardens — having access to local knowledge is just invaluable.'

They also recommend growing as much as you can from seed. They've observed that everything they have grown from seed seems to do so much better than bought seedlings. They concede it's more effort, and involves planning well ahead, but cultivating your own seedlings enables you to select the strongest plants, and gives you a better chance of a bumper crop.

NGAHERE: THE FOREST

While the edible garden was the main focus for Lucy and Jacob for the first few months, it wasn't long before they felt a pull from the surrounding bush. Regenerating the native forest through predator control and restoration planting using eco-sourced seedlings is now their greatest ambition.

They were lucky enough to inherit some large established canopy trees such as beech, rewarewa and tānekaha, but smaller shrubs, grasses and groundcovers local to the area have until recently been scarce. Incredibly, given their almost suburban location, the bush understorey has been browsed out by red deer. Birds responsible for seed dispersal have also had their numbers diminished by predators such as possums and rats.

Lucy and Jacob have become dedicated trappers. Installing a deer fence is the next plan, and it will be a challenging job, as post holes in the uneven terrain will need to be hand-dug. The good news is Lucy's brother-in-law is a fencer.

The couple applied for an indigenous biodiversity grant from the Hutt City Council in 2021. This offers up to $20,000 to a project that improves the biodiversity of a given location. If their application succeeds, the council will connect them with an ecologist who will talk to them about their biodiversity goals and help them make a plan.

Eventually Jacob and Lucy would love to build a small cabin in the bush, with views across the valley. With any luck, by then, a diverse understorey will be thriving under the canopy trees, the sound of tūī louder than ever.

NOTES FROM JACOB AND LUCY

PLANTING AND GROWING NATIVES

Based on our experience, we've put together a step-by-step guide to selecting and planting natives that are ecologically appropriate for your property.

Research to select the right plants
Despite what you may assume, not all native plants are suitable for your area. Your local council can supply a list of those that are.

When you have such a list, you need to choose those plants that will thrive in the conditions of your property. All plants have preferences in relation to shade, sun, wind, moisture and temperature.

Our list of native plants that thrive in Lower Hutt includes:

TREES: Five-finger, lancewood, lemonwood, lowland ribbonwood, māhoe, marbleleaf, tree hebe, beech, tōtara, miro, rimu

SHRUBS: *Alseuosmia pusilla*, *Coprosma rhamnoides*, *Coprosma rigida*, poataniwha, kawakawa (shade)

CLIMBERS: *Clematis paniculata*

GRASSES: Silver tussock (*Poa cita*)

FERNS: black tree fern, hen and chicken fern, kiokio, *Adiantum cunninghamii*, crown fern

Eco-sourcing
Make sure you check with your local nursery that the plants you are looking to buy are eco-sourced from your area. This means they have been bred locally and evolved to withstand local conditions. The same species planted in Canterbury and Wellington will behave slightly differently. The Wellington-born native will have been grown to withstand wind, for one thing!

Planting

Once you have selected the site, prepare it by removing all weeds. Native plants don't compete favourably with invasive weeds for moisture and nutrients, so try to remove as many as possible around the area.

Dig a square hole twice as wide and deep as the pot. Digging a square hole encourages the plant's roots to grow outwards as they reach the corners.

Half-fill the hole with compost, soil and some organic fertiliser. Place the plant in the hole and backfill. Water thoroughly.

Pest control

We have a huge issue with pests in Lower Hutt. Deer, possums, rats, pigs — we have to protect our natives from being browsed out of existence. We use two forms of exclusion: perimeter fencing and localised fencing (building protection around individual plants).

Trapping is also essential where we are. We use Timms possum traps and Goodnature A24 Rat & Mouse Traps at very tight (40-metre) spacings.

BIRCH HILL FLOWER FARM

Nicky's greenhouse is bursting at the seams with seedlings. Nigella, snapdragons and Queen Anne's lace are among the flowers that crane newly sprouted necks towards the windows. They are destined for one of the 21 flower beds that line Nicky's rural Okuku property in North Canterbury.

Birch Hill Flower Farm is easy to miss from the road — tucked in among sheep and beef farms. Yet turn down the drive and you are greeted by a painter's palette of flowers, featuring blooms of every hue.

It takes a bird's eye view to fully appreciate the 2000 square metres (half an acre) of 15-metre-long flower beds, all planted by Nicky. And she grows almost everything from seed, other than tubers and bulbs. In a world where flowers are often mass produced, sprayed with synthetic pesticides and flown thousands of kilometres across the globe, Nicky prefers to live life in the slow lane. Her kaupapa is cut flowers that are lovingly hand-grown in season, using organic principles where possible. Her happy blooms are supplied to florists, incorporated into bouquets she creates for her roadside stall, cut for her floral workshops and used in wedding arrangements.

Flower farming is not a bed of roses — there's a huge amount of work involved at every stage. Improving soil health has been a big challenge over the past three years, and Nicky also holds down a full-time day job. Yet hands in the soil, tending to her 40-plus varieties of flowers, is her happy place. She can't imagine herself doing anything else.

Half the interest of a garden is the constant exercise of the imagination. You are always living three, or indeed six, months hence. I believe that people entirely devoid of imagination never can be really good gardeners. To be content with the present, and not striving about the future, is fatal.

— MRS C. W. EARLE, *POT-POURRI FROM A SURREY GARDEN*, 1897

ABOUT THE GARDENER

Nicky's green thumb seems to have skipped a generation, as it's her grandparents who mostly feature in her early garden memories. She grew up in Waitahuna, a small Otago town. Her grandparents lived across the road on a farm and both were passionate about gardening. Her grandfather loved trees, especially conifers; while her grandmother's passion was flowers, particularly irises. Nicky thinks she owes her own love of flowers to her grandmother.

Nicky created green spaces wherever she rented, digging small gardens, planting herbs and dotting marigolds around her vegetables. Even a humble garden gave back so much more than the produce she harvested, enabling her to put down roots wherever she found herself. It was good for the soul. Nicky's gardens always gave her a sense of being grounded — while studying for a Bachelor of Science and later when raising her children, Sammie and Gibson, now young adults.

She's long loved the idea of an English country-style garden, complete with densely planted herbaceous borders, narrow paths and terraces. Even in her small gardens she would apply the conventions of the cottage garden, with smaller plants at the front and larger at the back, a bit of formality strategically placed among the whimsy.

While she worked as an insurance broker for nine years, flower farming was not at the forefront of Nicky's mind. But it was scrolling on Pinterest during the 2020 lockdown that sparked the idea of having her own flower farm. Stumbling across various flower farms online, she fell down the rabbit hole, pawing over all the beautiful farms and mulling the possibilities. Something about all those rows of flowers drew her in and she realised

that this path could satisfy her need for a creative outlet and her love of gardening.

She dove into research, spending hours on YouTube watching other growers' farm tours and tips; scouring her local library for books on anything flower-related. When she decided to take the plunge, she was in boots and all, literally. She decided to specialise in the more boutique and heirloom varieties that florists cannot import as they don't ship well.

At the time, Nicky was renting the house on the 4-hectare Birch Hill property. She spoke to her landlord about creating a 'small' flower garden, and he gave his nod of approval. Nicky broke the news to her partner, then broke ground. She created six flower beds in that first season, and shortly afterwards they bought the property, so there was no stopping her.

It was the first time Nicky had attempted any gardening project on this scale — having free reign was a foreign concept and slightly daunting, but the opportunities that lay ahead were intoxicating.

The farm's stony land proved a huge challenge from the start, as did the howling nor'west wind that often blows across Canterbury. She recalls much trial and error, endless reading, hours spent on YouTube. She would try things, fail, research some more, try again and eventually her effort would begin to pay off.

Through all of this, Nicky has continued in her full-time insurance job, working on her flower farm before and after work and on weekends. It's incredibly busy and a constant race against daylight, eking the most out of every day. To make best use of her time she has become a self-confessed 'crazy diary lady', with two diaries running parallel. But it works. This precision planning means the whole venture runs like clockwork. She knows when seeds need to be ordered, what needs to be sown when, when seedlings will be ready to transplant — ensuring a steady crop of flowers ready to harvest across the growing season. She finds the physical nature of the work, the birdsong, and getting her hands in the soil provide a welcome change at the end of a day in the office.

ABOUT THE GARDEN

Nicky's flower farm is a 15-minute drive from Rangiora, en route to Ashley Gorge. The house on Birch Hill Farm was built in 1995. When they arrived, there were established trees around the house and in the garden, and under them were some massively overgrown hebes. Nicky pulled these out and underplanted the trees with hostas, little box hedges and shade-loving perennials, experimenting with different textures such as Japanese forest grass, trillium and maples. The biggest job, requiring arduous effort, has been to remediate the soil on the former riverbed. An enormous number of rocks and stones have been removed, and vast quantities of mushroom compost brought in.

In her first season she planted the original 6 × 10-metre beds with a selection of heirloom varieties including dahlias, zinnias, snapdragons, bells of Ireland, mignonette, straw flowers and amaranthus. That year she grew the seedlings inside on her windowsills, splashing out on a 3 × 3-metre greenhouse in her second season. Three tiers of shelves were crammed full with seedlings from June until her last planting in January. That year she got to work digging 16 beds 15 metres long, to accommodate all the seedlings. As demand from florists grew, so did Nicky's ambition, and a second greenhouse, double the size of the first, was built in 2022.

Everything she grows needs to have a good vase life, and also needs to be 'on trend' — what florists are looking for. Nostalgia is a huge factor in the current popularity of the heritage varieties, and Nicky enjoys the magic of the way a single bloom can reignite memories from childhood, or transport someone back to their grandmother's garden.

Against a backdrop of climate change and the contribution that toxic chemicals make to the problem, Nicky is an avid promoter of the 'slow flower' movement. She uses no commercial sprays and all her flowers are seasonally grown. She applies mushroom compost in spring and autumn, in the belief that healthy soil creates healthy plants in a healthy environment.

Initially she adopted the chop 'n' drop method, chopping up spent stems and foliage and spreading them as mulch around the farm, to be incorporated naturally back into the soil. However, experience taught her that this organic material could become a breeding ground for diseases before it broke down sufficiently, so these days all her green waste is composted — she grew pumpkins in the compost pile this year.

Around the pond beside the flower beds Nicky has planted 18 willow trees, the goal being to harvest the branches for basket and wreath making, both of which she teaches in workshops. Near them is a newly planted shelterbelt of ninebark, *Acacia baileyana* 'Purpurea', eucalyptus and birch. She loves the look of the white papery bark of the birch set against the blue-purple tinge of the acacia.

A small weatherboard studio has been built at the edge of the site, overlooking the flower garden. Nicky is a keen painter (when she can find the time) and her dream is to be able to paint botanical works in her studio through winter.

Over the coming year she plans to put in some raised beds to grow shoulder-season varieties such as heirloom chrysanthemums. To ease the workload, Nicky has employed a friend to help her pick one day a week. She can now enjoy the work of cutting and harvesting rather than worrying the whole time about the sun dipping out of sight before she is finished. Students from the local floristry schools in Christchurch and Lincoln University have also come on board as interns and for work experience. Nicky appreciates the help, and the knowledge trade has been invaluable for both parties.

Nicky says her next focus is to get smarter about how she operates — flipping beds and using them all the time instead of letting them sit idle. Her goal is to utilise every piece of dirt to its full capacity, to be as productive as possible on her small plot. She plans to build up an English-style long border display garden, and eventually to offer the property as a wedding venue. Portuguese laurels are already growing and beginning to set the scene.

Her advice to anyone thinking of heading down this path is just do it, but start small. 'The more I do, the more capable I feel. I pride myself on the quality of my flowers, and it's just such good therapy having your hands in the dirt. Nurturing baby plants and seeing them come to fruition, seeing the joy they bring people; I'm in love with the whole process.'

NOTES FROM NICKY

GROWING FROM SEED

I germinate my seeds in three ways:

1. In cell trays in the greenhouse.
2. In plastic milk bottles (see below). This is a great method for hardy annual seeds.
3. Direct in the field. Some plants, such as bells of Ireland, larkspur and orlaya white lace, can be more successful if direct sown, though I often sow these in cell trays so I can maintain control over spacing.

HARDY ANNUALS: I germinate hardy annual seeds in late winter so they can be planted out in the field in early spring, before the last frost. They are not only tolerant of the cold but thrive in cooler temperatures. Examples are snapdragons, annual scabiosa, bells of Ireland, larkspur, Queen Anne's lace, sweet peas, corncockle.

HEAT-LOVING ANNUALS: These plants love the heat of summer but don't tolerate frost, so I germinate them a bit later and plant out in the field after the threat of frost has passed. Try zinnias, amaranthus, annual aster, celosia, sunflowers, cosmos.

Germinating hardy annuals in milk bottles
- Halfway down a 2-litre milk bottle, make a horizontal cut around three sides, leaving enough uncut so that it forms a 'hinge'.
- Poke holes in the bottom of the bottle for drainage, and a few in the top part for air flow.
- Fill the bottom of the bottle with about 10 centimetres damp seed-raising mix.
- Plant the seeds as directed on the packet. A good rule of thumb is to sow at a depth twice the size of the seed. You can plant them fairly densely, as you'll be dividing them up to transplant in spring.

- Spray the surface with water so the top layer is quite damp.
- Label a stick and poke it into the soil — it's less likely to fade than if you write the name on the bottle.
- Put the lid on and duct-tape the bottle closed all the way around. Place it outside and let Mother Nature do the rest.
- You can leave the plastic cap on until the seeds germinate. This will keep the moisture in and hasten germination.
- Once the seeds germinate, remove the cap to allow rain to get in and air to circulate.

✦ ✦ ✦

THE CHELSEA CHOP

The term comes from the UK, because growers do it in preparation for the annual Chelsea Flower Show in May. It involves cutting back your perennials by a half to a third to extend their flowering, and in New Zealand it is done in late spring or early summer. Flowers such as mignonette will rebloom after a good cut-back; others will simply flower better and for longer. Phlox, aster and sedum will not grow so leggy if cut back prior to their first flush. Examples of other summer- and autumn-flowering perennials that respond to this pruning method are penstemon, goldenrod, yarrow, campanula and rudbeckia.

✦ ✦ ✦

NOSTALGIC BLOOMS FOR THE PICKING GARDEN

One of the first (and most fun!) steps towards realising my flower farm dream was to research and select what I would actually grow. My vision was to specialise in the sort of nostalgic, cottagey blooms that you would expect to find in granny's garden but of course there were lots of practical considerations that had to be factored in — what will florists want to buy/what are the current trends? Will it grow well in my location and climate? How well does it travel, and how long will it last in a vase? And so on.

With each new season I refine and expand my plant selection as my knowledge grows, and as new plots are developed for planting. Here is a small selection of some of my favourite blooms, ideal for the home 'picking garden'.

Achillea 'Colorado Mix'

Achillea 'The Pearl'

Amaranthus cruentus (red amaranth)

Antirrhinum majus 'Madame Butterfly Mix'

Buddleia (butterfly bush)

Buddleia (butterfly bush)

Centaurea cyanus (cornflower)

Cerinthe major (honeywort)

Consolida ajacis (larkspur)

CORNWALL POCKET FARM

On a compact 300-square-metre section in suburban Onehunga, Tāmaki Makaurau Auckland, Jenny has created a little gem of a garden that is not only earth-friendly and highly productive but an enchanting Mediterranean-style living space.

In 2019 Jenny and her husband Mark embarked on a bold lifestyle overhaul. In response to the daunting reality of climate breakdown, biodiversity loss and pollution, they resolved to become part of the solution, not the problem. The extent of her gardening experience thus far had been a grow pod on her apartment balcony, but Jenny saw this as an invigorating challenge rather than a deterrent, and she launched herself into watching endless gardening videos to figure out what she wanted to grow and how to do it.

Realising that it is more sustainable for people to live in cities, Jenny decided to create a small but productive urban farm. She recognised that we can't all go bush or there would be no room left for the wildlife. These days her job title is 'Earth Worker at Cornwall Pocket Farm'. She is passionate about enabling and inspiring others to make a difference in their own back yard and would love to see other 'pocket farms' popping up throughout the city. To that end she has set up her own YouTube channel, 'Cornwall Pocket Farm', to document her journey of figuring out how to live sustainably on 300 square metres in the city.

The greatest lesson that climate change is forcing on us is that rather than changing the way that we do the same thing we need to rethink what we do, literally from the ground up.

— MONTY DON

ABOUT THE GARDENER

Originally from the UK, Jenny and Mark moved to Aotearoa 30 years ago and raised their two daughters here. On their return from a year cycling around Europe, they rented a city apartment in Auckland while looking for a house to buy. Jenny installed a planter on the apartment deck and tried growing a few vegetables from seedlings she'd picked up from the hardware store . . . with mixed results.

Her sustainability journey began in 2016 when she saw a video online. It was so extreme she thought perhaps it was a spoof, but it wasn't. It was an interview with *The Guardian*'s environmental columnist George Monbiot, discussing the climate crisis. In 2013 Monbiot wrote:

> The extreme events to which climate change appears to have contributed reflect an average rise in global temperatures of 0.6° C over the past century. The consensus among climatologists is that temperatures will rise in the 21st century by between 1.4 and 5.8° C: by up to 10 times, in other words, the increase we have suffered so far . . . We are not contemplating the end of holidays in Seville. We are contemplating the end of the circumstances which permit most human beings to remain on Earth.

A little digging and Jenny found Monbiot's reporting to be scientifically rigorous and reliable. She was horrified.

The house hunt took on a new objective: to find not just a house and garden, but a new way of living that would positively affect climate change from their own back yard.

Jenny and Mark bought a small suburban 1950s house and spent a year

retrofitting it to be energy and water efficient, with low emissions. This retrofit involved a lot of insulation, harnessing the sun's energy through passive solar design, double glazing, and a large rainwater tank for use in the house and garden. To completely change how they were living, though, Jenny knew she needed to incorporate a garden. Growing their own food would cut out food miles, chemical fertilisers and pesticides, and circumvent the impacts of industrial agriculture.

Having a background in graphic design and education, most recently as education manager for the Green Building Council, Jenny conducted extensive research to find creative solutions. She learned that there are six key categories in everyday living that impact the environment, each of which needs to be drastically reimagined in order to reach sustainability goals: water, waste, energy, transport, consumption and food. The house and garden design would hugely reduce their water and energy consumption, and, having lived in Europe without a car, selling their vehicle was a no-brainer. Jenny walks, uses public transport, and rents a car if she needs one.

When it came to the garden, Jenny felt she was really starting from scratch. She spent a year watching gardening videos, learning the practical skills of vegetable growing and garden design, soil health and companion planting, with the overarching goal of feeding themselves in collaboration with nature.

Three years on, she has not only built a beautiful, productive garden that feeds her and Mark as well as the birds and insects, but she has also built an exceptional depth and breadth of gardening knowledge. Having looked online for a local gardening group without any luck, she started one with a group of neighbourhood gardening enthusiasts who now meet every month to talk about gardening and visit other people's gardens.

Of course none of this happened overnight. It was, and is, a long-term project, but one that has been easier, more affordable and more rewarding than Jenny ever imagined. She's passionate about creating a transferable model for making many small changes to the way we live in order to create impactful change. We *can* all live differently. It's not only possible but urgent and vital for us to do so. Making changes to how we consume goods, manage household waste and create food security doesn't mean changing who we are, it means working creatively and collaboratively to live differently in our urban environments.

Jenny has quit her day job to focus on her garden, which is possible because their new lifestyle is so much cheaper than their old one. They consume less power and water, they've ditched the car and changed their consumer behaviour, and the garden is now their main source of fresh food. Jenny does an online grocery shop every couple of months to stock the pantry, and Mark harvests dinner each evening from the garden. They have both also become vegetarian, to further reduce their carbon emissions. (Although they will eat meat if they're out for dinner, and occasionally satisfy a craving for sausages!)

A new phase of Jenny's project to live differently is emerging out of her background in education and passion for environmental action. Her YouTube channel, 'Cornwall Pocket Farm', now has dozens of videos, featuring tours of her garden and instructional clips on how to grow tomatoes, how to make bread, and building fly traps. Sharing what she's learned, and growing her reach by opening the garden to curious visitors, is the next chapter in her project.

ABOUT THE GARDEN

When Jenny and Mark bought the property it consisted of a lawn, three enormous conifers, a single fig tree and a lot of concrete. Jenny drew a bird's-eye-view plan, using the fig tree and fence as reference points, and has since planted another 25 trees, a productive kitchen garden, a grape-covered pergola, a rambling corner of berries and wildflowers, climbing roses and natives. She has also built a wildlife pond, an insect hotel and a chicken coop for her four laying hens — all on 200 square metres. Every centimetre is utilised.

Planning as if looking down from above the garden afforded much more space than Jenny had initially imagined when she was standing at the gate. Her inspiration for the design came from the garden of a great-aunt whose English Victorian estate, and particularly the kitchen gardens, were a childhood playground for Jenny. She was also attracted to the many potagers she admired while cycling through Europe.

Her starting point for the potager was, and always is, deciding what they want to eat (not radishes!), so they're never doing big harvests unless it's fruit for preserving. They eat whatever is in season. The next step was gathering the knowledge of what these things need to grow — learning about soil conditions, companion planting, watering and hours of sunlight. Jenny's plan accounted for shade cover from trees, which are primarily on parallel edges of the property, and plotted four central kitchen garden beds in the sunniest spots. Down one side of the house is the utilities area with the washing line, rainwater tank, pump and waste bins, and down the other are brambles and berries that require less sun and don't mind the poorer soil in this part of the garden.

Wanting a range of fruit trees to provide food throughout the year, Jenny researched extensively, both appropriate species and growing techniques for saving space. In the chicken coop, to provide shade for the chooks, are four avocado trees planted together in a cubic-metre planter. The plan is that this 'family planting' will ensure effective cross-pollination, providing them with avocados for most of the year.

Wanting apples for a variety of uses and seasons, Jenny planted cooking, eating, early and late varieties, with the same diversity for pears. These are grown in espalier form, creating a hedge along one side of the kitchen garden. Jenny ordered double-grafted trees, which arrived with bare roots and needing to be chopped down very low but above the graft. New branches would grow from those points, and Jenny continues to chop wherever new branches are needed. This kind of extreme pruning keeps the trees small but produces great quantities of fruit.

Tangerine, lime and orange trees fill a citrus grove, and a micro food forest against a fence includes dwarf Cavendish bananas, a particularly productive elder tree, plums, lemongrass, wild strawberries, rhubarb and rambling passionfruit vines.

There's always food coming out of the kitchen garden. Most seasons, each of the four beds has a couple of priority crops: tomatoes in summer for their versatility in relishes and pasta sauce, beans for their heavy cropping and because they freeze so well, pumpkins as they're so easy to grow and store well, courgettes because they're great producers.

Around these 'hero' vegetables Jenny plants many different crops. It doesn't look as neat as classic rows of vegetables, but it works better, she says. If the goal is to feed yourself, it's more productive to have a diverse range of vegetables providing constant ground cover. Little plants pop in between bigger plants so they are sheltered as they mature, and no crop rotation is required as everything is intermingled. This method of planting results in a variety of food every day, without a huge glut of, say, cabbages that go on for weeks.

Just as we do, soil biota — bacteria, fungi, algae and soil animals — thrive on a diverse diet, which is hindered by mono-crop planting. The symbiotic relationship between plants and soil in a varied garden provides a greater variety of nutrients to soil life, which in turn provides better nutrition to the plants. Healthy soil is also a vital component in regulating carbon. Monbiot quotes a 2014 UK study showing that 'soil in allotments — the small patches in towns and cities that people cultivate by hand — contains a third more organic

carbon than agricultural soil and 25% more nitrogen . . . [and] produce[s] between four and 11 times more food per hectare than do farmers'.

Jenny uses the no-dig approach, pioneered by horticulturalist Charles Dowding. Rather than digging over a patch of garden prior to planting, you simply pile a layer of compost on top, and plant into that. Soil microorganisms do the rest. According to gardener and writer Monty Don, whose gardening videos Jenny has devoured, there are more living organisms in the first six inches of the soil than there are stars in the known universe. Left to their own devices, these organisms will work to create healthy, productive soil. By contrast, industrial agriculture's planting of vast areas in mono crops and use of synthetic fertilisers and pesticides are enormously detrimental to soil health and ecosystems, and one of the greatest contributors to climate change.

Jenny describes everything in the garden as a wonderful challenge — challenging herself to learn and find creative, low-impact solutions to problems. But she also accepts that if something doesn't grow, it just doesn't. You just pull it out and move on. She's learning what grows well in her garden, how much she needs to plant, and the best plan for garden maintenance. Ever a fastidious planner, she devised a spreadsheet for recording what she had done in the garden and using this information to plan ahead. Jenny's spreadsheets calculate seed germination and maturation times, meaning she can ensure she has a diverse range of food available to her throughout the year.

Anything Jenny needs for the garden is scavenged or recycled. Initially, the house renovation provided masses of rimu that was repurposed for the vegetable beds and central climbing structure, named Crystal Palace. The torn-down carport was refashioned into the chicken coop, Henley Hall, and old concrete went into retaining walls to flatten part of the garden area that had been on a slope. Jenny collects grass clippings and her neighbours' wool insulation from food-box deliveries to use as mulch, and a bird cage found on the roadside performs perfectly as a cloche for protecting small natives in the chicken coop.

Jenny has named her four kitchen garden beds after European countries — England and Germany for the fence-side beds that get less sun, Italy and France for the two beds nearer the house that receive the most sun. In her spreadsheets, each 'country' is divided into regions or cities denoting areas for particular plant groups.

The palpable sense of humour, creativity, experimentation and discovery evident in Cornwall Pocket Farm reflect Jenny and Mark's personalities.

They might be overhauling their lives to make real, practical moves towards sustainable living, but they're still themselves, and they're having fun. They haven't lost or sacrificed anything; on the contrary, they have gained enormous knowledge and genuine enjoyment in making an ever-expanding series of exciting small changes.

It's a work in progress: the garden is always changing, no year is ever the same as the last. In the first year as Earth Worker at Cornwall Pocket Farm, Jenny joked that she was self-sufficient in garnishes. Just three years on, she eats almost entirely from her small urban garden.

NOTES FROM JENNY

REUSING OLD CONCRETE

Old concrete, or 'urbanite' as it is also called, is a wonderful resource in the garden. An ugly old concrete path can (with a bit of effort) be transformed into a beautiful dry-stone retaining wall that is not only functional but creates a real feature in the garden, especially with trailing plants tumbling over the side. There is no need to add cement as it is self-supporting due to its weight, just like a traditional dry-stone wall.

Making an urbanite wall
Make sure the ground is level and firm, ideally using some sand or builders' gravel to achieve this.

Set up a string line along what will be the face of your wall at the height of your first layer. This will help you to keep the wall straight and each layer of concrete level (unless of course you want to make a curved wall!).

Lay your first layer of concrete pieces on the ground, keeping the side surface flat against the string. If you are making a retaining wall, you will only need to worry about the front surface as the back side will be hidden by soil. If you are building a free-standing wall, you will need to keep both sides flat.

Build up the wall layer by layer. Try to keep the top surface relatively level, although you can make some correction with each layer — a smaller piece on top of a larger piece in the previous layer will even the surface out.

If you're making a retaining wall you want to lay the concrete pieces so the wall slopes very slightly towards the soil bank. A few larger pieces that will extend into the soil bank behind the wall will help create stability.

If you're making a freestanding wall, build up two rows side by side, laying the edge pieces of concrete so they slope slightly towards the centre of the wall. Infill the centre with rubble and small broken pieces of concrete. As you work up the wall, include some pieces that straddle the entire width of the wall to increase stability.

The bottom layers should be a little wider and subsequent layers slightly narrower. You gradually reduce the width of the wall towards the top, while keeping it centred on the base. Keep moving the string up and adding new layers on top until you reach your desired height.

+ + +

FINDING SPACE IN A SMALL GARDEN

The best ways to find a bit of extra space are to:

- Look at your garden with a bird's eye view
- Think about your garden three-dimensionally — up as well as out
- Train your plants to grow in the space you have, e.g. low horizontal espalier growing.

I find it really helpful to draw a scale plan of the garden. I mark in the existing structures and planting, and then look at what space is left. A primary requirement for plants is light, so any space that gets light can be planted. If it's a hard surface, think about adding pots or a raised bed. Many plants, both edible and ornamental, are happy in pots — even small trees if the container is large enough.

The other place to find space is 'up'. Think about creating structures in your garden, up which you can grow your plants. This is also a great idea for adding seasonal shade in hot summers. A bamboo wigwam takes up little space in your garden bed but will produce a lot of peas or beans in that limited space. Or you can get more creative with permanent structures that add height and interest to your garden and can be used to grow all manner of climbing plants, annual and perennial. Hanging baskets are another option to add that little bit of extra space in the sun.

I use a lot of different training techniques to maximise fruit trees in the small space I have. I fan-train some trees, or use a more formal espalier method. This requires a structure that you can tie the branches to, then you train the tree into your required shape by pruning off any growth that is going the wrong way. You have to be quite strict with the trees but they will reward you with more fruit, they will live longer, and they are a lot easier to cover with netting if you need to protect your precious crop from the birds.

I have also planted a few 'step-over' fruit trees that are only 60 centimetres tall. They are essentially just very short espalier trees with only one tier allowed to grow — a bit like Bonsai but not quite that extreme... and you get fruit!

+ + +

SLUG BAIT RECIPE

This is what I use to preserve my tender new seedlings from slugs in spring when the ground is moist. This recipe will make enough to fill four small bowls, which I dig into the garden bed so the lip is level with the soil. Slugs love the stuff!

3 cups water
3 teaspoons sugar
3 teaspoons flour
1½ teaspoons dried yeast

Add all ingredients to a jar and shake well. Pour into your partly submerged containers to about 1 centimetre below the top, so the slugs can dive in easily but can't get out. You can then just empty the containers into your compost every few days (or after rain), and set up a new batch. Cheap, organic and effective!

I use a digital removal method for the snails and caterpillars that try to eat my brassicas... I just pick them off with my 'digits' (i.e. by hand) and 'rehome' them in the chicken coop.

TEXTURE GARDEN

Sue's Texture Garden is a collection of subtropical, native and unusual plants that has been her labour of love for the past 30 years.

The garden's 2000 square metres (half an acre) was subdivided from a farm, and she and husband Hamish live in the original 1910 farmhouse, where they raised their family. Sue once came across a letter written by a woman who grew up in the house, which describes being a child at the local primary school during the 1931 Napier earthquake. Her father rode down to collect her from the school on his horse.

The colonial township of Taradale, now considered a suburb of Napier, developed in a piecemeal, unplanned fashion, not unlike the evolution of Sue's garden. She has never had a design as such, because her interests, knowledge, discoveries and plant collection are continually evolving.

... the things we choose to look at in life loom large, changing the version of reality we live in, whether it's cars or fashion or the natural world. Knowing one bird from another tells me how many species are around me, populating my urban world with their lives; learning about trees has made my city greener, because my eye no longer passes over them as though they were hardly there. If you live in a city and miss 'nature', the answer doesn't have to be to move out; it's to tune in.

— MELISSA HARRISON, *THE STUBBORN LIGHT OF THINGS: A NATURE DIARY*

ABOUT THE GARDENER

Sue would be the first to admit she is obsessed with plants. She describes it as a deep love for everything about them: their texture, beauty, colour, smell. But it's more than that, too — she is fascinated by the relationship we have with plants, our cohabitation, the fact that we couldn't live without them.

Sue grew up just around the corner, when the area was semi-rural, and her childhood was spent outdoors, largely in the paddling pool and sandpit. Sue's mum always gardened but, especially in the early days, her focus was on flowers more than food. Despite the fact that she was raising six children, there were always cut flowers in the house. The family grew some green vegetables and had citrus trees, and otherwise bought produce from the local market garden. Sue's father often traded his GP services for produce, including eggs, cream and real milk that came in mason jars.

House plants were Sue's first plant obsession. Her bedroom in her student flat was full of them. Then she went travelling, and house plants went out of fashion. It wasn't until Sue and Hamish bought their own house that gardening really opened up for her. Their first home was high on a Wellington hill and this garden was literally a steep learning curve for Sue. They were only there for a couple of years. She grew flowers and planted many natives that didn't survive the exposed conditions.

It was during this time that she began to become obsessed with plant books. She devoured library books — and still does. The foundation of her gardening knowledge comes from books and magazines, and her fascination with plants grew alongside. So when she and Hamish moved back to Napier in 1990 and were looking to buy a home for their young family, it was the garden she fell in love with.

They arrived in Hawke's Bay on a Friday, and on Saturday morning Sue's mum saw the property listed in the local paper. Sue remembers driving down to the house — an old villa that had had some questionable work done on it over the years — and not even looking inside. What she saw was the garden, a sylvan setting of established exotic trees on an expansive sunny section.

They bought the property, put up a fence to keep the kids in, built a tree hut, took down the net curtains, and Sue threw herself into the garden.

Slowly she began to meet others who loved plants as much as she did. Sometimes she and her friends would make garden-visit road trips throughout Te Ika-a-Māui, the North Island, while Hamish held the fort at home.

One garden they visited, which has remained one of Sue's inspirations, was Gordon Collier's Taihape garden set in the bush. Collier, a landscaper and expert in unusual plants, now in his eighties, structured his garden around mature trees — maple, silver birch and redwood — within which lie a series of distinct gardens designed around foliage shape, texture and seasonal colour. Ayrlies Garden in east Auckland was another early influence for Sue. In an informal style it merges subtropicals and natives with the scale and drama of a country estate.

Much of Sue's tropical and subtropical plant discoveries have been inspired by Russell Fransham's nursery in Whangārei, and Nicki and Clive Higgie's Paloma Gardens in Fordell, 20 kilometres from Whanganui. Fransham specialised in tropical and unusual plants, importing species and swapping among his community of plant enthusiasts to build an exceptionally diverse collection. Paloma is an eccentric, surprising garden with a similarly diverse collection of mostly exotic plants, including a desert garden, a sculpture collection and large-scale plantings of peculiar specimens.

Natives have always been one of Sue's obsessions, but discovering these local gardens that work with the Aotearoa climate and landscape to grow surprising tropical and subtropical plants has deeply informed her own gardening.

When her three children were school-aged, Sue worked at a local plant nursery. Over those seven years she developed a detailed knowledge of propagation, and gardening in alignment with the lunar cycle. She would advise customers on starting a garden from bare land on a lifestyle block, or wanting shelter for their houses in hot, dry conditions. She progressed from there to independently practising garden design for Hawke's Bay clients. Her plant knowledge now is encyclopaedic.

Sue's other passion is floral art. A longtime member and past president of the local floral art group, she has presented numerous demonstrations and workshops, and designed flowers for all sorts of events and weddings — including a wedding in Umbria, Italy, which took place in a fourteenth-century villa. In her floristry practice Sue loves pushing the boundaries of what can be achieved with foliage and natural products. She enjoys applying the floral art principles of balance, form, texture, colour and proportion in her garden, and in turn taking inspiration from her garden for her floral designs.

ABOUT THE GARDEN

Sue's Texture Garden is a series of almost theatrical encounters. Some are micro, like the acid pink, violet-tipped baubles of the Brazilian matchstick bromeliad, or the silver spiderwebs strung taut between spiky air plants growing from the plateau of a punga stump. Some encounters are macro — slatted nīkau blades explode from a tumble of frothy Japanese silver grass; punga trees frame an enormous fern, its illuminated feathers sliced by harakeke shadows. Each scene is a playful composition of textures, colour and proportion.

The garden changes form over the seasons and has morphed over the years. It's a space of experimentation, play and enjoyment for Sue, who hasn't set out to create a 'pretty' garden, but rather has focused on using unusual plants to create spaces to live in: a sunny morning porch, a subtropical walk, a herb garden, a dry hot bank, a games lawn, a native track and an afternoon dining area. Large trees, both the original plantings and the others planted by Sue, provide structure to the garden design, as well as forming integral components of textural compositions.

Sue and Hamish kept what mature trees they could, removing only unhealthy ones, as well as a Norfolk Island hibiscus whose fibrous stamens irritate the skin like fibreglass. In its place, Hamish built a treehouse. The property's previous owner of many decades was a passionate gardener, and her redwood and ginkgo now tower over the property. The gingko — a male plant that doesn't produce the malodorous fruit that females do — is one of only a few deciduous trees in the garden. Come autumn, it produces dramatic splotches of yellow, umber and crimson.

While the trees produce a lot of shade — increasingly so as Sue's additions mature — this has opened up opportunities she can work with. The shelter they provide has enabled the planting of more and more subtropical species, which in turn has established microclimates in the garden that defuse the crisp Hawke's Bay frosts. The garden is mostly flat with an almost imperceivable incline, is predominantly north facing, and the soil is loamy — a free-draining, fertile sand–silt–clay composition that is conducive to growing a diversity of plant life in constructed conditions (the home garden, as opposed to a rainforest 'in the wild').

Sue suspects her soil is more alkaline than acidic, as she's never had much luck growing blue hydrangeas, even with the addition of alum salts to shift the soil pH levels. Fighting nature isn't part of her gardening ideology anyway, and she's happy with pink hydrangeas.

Old-fashioned roses were another of her all-consuming plant obsessions for a while, and she had over a hundred at one stage. Now she's down to three, kept for sentimental reasons: a cutting taken from her family home before her parents sold it, a hybrid that one of her ancestors bred, and one named 'My Mum', a blush-coloured bushy rose in memory of her own mother. She's more relaxed too about her native area, which once contained exclusively endemic flora. Nowadays she doesn't mind some infiltration by exotics.

The textures of different plants are highlighted in compositions featuring contrasting plants. Young horoeka (lancewood) in small groupings extend serrated blades from their tender trunks. When the light is low in autumn, the delicate shedding of the paperbark tree ignites in the sunlight like the coppery exoskeleton of a cicada. The brushy upright stems of a foxtail fern are featured against the silhouettes of various aloe species — *Aloe speciosa* with its meaty grey tentacles; the horn-edged, reptile-like *A. arborescens* (candelabra aloe); and the strappy *A. thraskii* (dune aloe) with its yellow rosettes.

Perhaps most intriguing of all Sue's wonderfully peculiar plants is the silk floss tree (not to be confused with a silk tree). Native to the subtropical forests of South America, it produces pink flossy blossoms and hand-like leaves of five or so leaflets. But it's the solid cylindrical trunk that is the modest focal point of a corner of Sue's garden. Between the armoured trunk of a punga and the weeping branchlets of a rimu, the trunk is illuminated, almost silver, and pocked with uniform thorny protrusions. The silk floss tree's thorns are otherworldly, reminiscent of pufferfish scales or ancient reptile skin, an anomaly even in this garden of textural curiosities.

For all its many wonders and encounters, there's something relaxed about Sue's Texture Garden. Its domestic scale and the smaller spaces she's created within it make it approachable; they're extensions of the rooms in the house, made to experience and enjoy.

Sue is not a fussy gardener. If something dies, well, it just didn't work in that space. She doesn't irrigate or spray, often forgets to use rooting hormone for propagation, and the lawn turns brown in summer because that's just what nature does. Any watering needed she does with a hose, listening to the shining cuckoo, grey warblers and bellbirds around her.

Sue read somewhere that gardening is the slowest of the performing arts, a constantly evolving interaction. Her favourite spot to watch the show unfold is from a comfy old sofa on the porch.

NOTES FROM SUE

PROPAGATION BY CUTTINGS AND DIVISION

Growing your own plants from scratch gives you a real sense of achievement as well as saving money.

These are the propagation steps I follow.

Cuttings

Plants that are usually easy to propagate this way include hebes, hydrangeas, roses, rosemary, daisies, chrysanthemums, geraniums, lavender and buxus. Not all will strike, but most do.

The best time to take a cutting is when you're standing in front of the plant — just do it! It's good to do this when there is a full moon because the sap is at its highest in the stems, meaning the plants are in their best condition. However, I'm happy to take cuttings at any time, especially if I won't be back at that site again.

If you're not going to pot them up straight away (perhaps you're visiting from out of town), wrap the stem ends in wet tissue or paper towel and place them in a plastic bag. As soon as you get home, preferably within a day or so, unwrap them to allow them to breathe, and pop them in cool water while you prepare your pot. Don't let them dry out.

The best cuttings are tip ends that include 3 or 4 sets of leaves. Strip off the bottom 2 sets, and also cut the remaining leaves in half if they are large, such as hydrangeas, to reduce moisture loss.

Using a stick or pencil to make holes, insert the end into a half-and-half mixture of potting mix and sand. Ensure there are two or more sets of leaf nodes below the surface. You may wish to dip the ends in hormone rooting powder first but I don't usually bother. Good drainage is important, but no fertiliser is required at this stage.

Insert the stems around the outside edge of the pot, and one in the centre. I have found that the cuttings near the edge of the pot do better, as when their roots reach the side of the pots they grow down, promoting strong roots.

Leave them for a few weeks, or months if it's winter. Water well — twice daily in hot temperatures — and keep in the shade in summer.

In spring, or when roots have formed, pot each cutting into a clean pot with fresh potting mix. Water well, keep it out of the sun until it's growing, then add fertiliser and gradually reintroduce it to sun.

Division

This method applies to plants that have strappy leaves, such as flax, liriope, mondo, rengarenga and wood irises.

Divide the root ball using a sharp spade or fork. Try to separate into sections, each with some roots attached. Trim off any dead leaves and excess foliage. With flax you only need to leave three leaves uncut.

Plant up a few bunches together in fresh potting mix. Water well and keep out of the sun until the plant recovers and starts growing. Fertilise a few weeks after it has settled in.

You can always try planting directly into your garden, but make sure you water daily for a week, especially in hot weather.

Bulbs, rhizomes and tubers

Here we're talking about irises, calla lilies, cannas, alstroemeria, taro, lilies and bluebells.

Dig up and gently prise apart a clump of bulbs/rhizomes/tubers to separate them, making sure you keep roots attached.

Discard anything dead or unhealthy-looking.

Replant separately in freshly worked soil with added compost and fertiliser or into pots of fresh potting mix. Ensure good drainage in both locations — bulbs hate wet feet.

Bulbs may be planted some way under the surface, but rhizomes and tubers like to be just under (or even on) the surface.

Add a stick label if you think you'll forget where you've planted them!

+ + +

SOME PLANTS IDEAL FOR FLORAL WORK

Aspidistra: A very hardy, long-lived plant that does well in shade. The leaves last well picked, and dry to a pale blond–rust colour.

Astelia chathamica: The silver leaves that are similar to small flax may be used straight or rolled and pinned.

Brachyglottis greyi: Hardy grey foliage that picks well for bouquets.

Camellia: Flowers of the large varieties float well in shallow water and the evergreen leaves are long-lasting. Great for pinning.

Fatsia japonica: The large palmate glossy green leaves last well picked, adding drama and a tropical look to designs.

Flax: Coming in various colours, flax leaves may be used fresh, rolled, plaited, shredded or dried. The seed pods and stalks (claddies) can also be used dried.

Hebes: There are so many species. The bigger-leaved types are good for bouquet fillers.

Hellebores: The flowers float well and pick well once they're starting to set seed. The leaves are also a useful contrast when combined with smaller-leaved material.

Hydrangeas: The flowers may be used fresh or dry, often adding beautiful antique colour.

Magnolia: Deciduous varieties often have stunning large bowl-like flowers in winter and furry buds on interesting stems. Evergreen varieties have glossy green leaves with tan suede-like backing. Very long-lived when picked, and they preserve well too.

Philodendron 'Xanadu': Small long-lobed leaves that pick well, adding a tropical look to designs.

Strelitzia reginae: Dramatic orange and blue flowers with large paddle-shaped leaves — both are great for adding drama.

Succulents: The rosette shapes of echeverias and aeoniums do especially well. They last a long time and may be planted back in the garden at the end!

PLANTS FOR FORM AND TEXTURE

My love of gardening is fuelled by my passion for plants. I marvel at their different forms, colours and textures, and love experimenting with placement and combinations. I especially love to observe how light plays on their leaves and bark, across the seasons and at different times of day.

I believe the best way to learn about plants is by close observation, by exploring and tuning into other gardens — private gardens, show gardens, botanic gardens or in nature. Carry a notebook, ask questions, take photos and take cuttings (with permission).

Here is a very small selection of some of the plants I've collected over the years. These bring me so much pleasure every day.

Acacia 'Limelight'

Acer dissectum

Acer griseum (paperback maple)

Acer palmatum 'Dissectum Atropurpureum' (Japanese maple)

Adiantum aethiopicum (maidenhair fern)

Aechmea gamosepala (matchstick bromeliad)

Ajania pacifica

Aloe speciosa

Aloe thraskii

GREENHILLS PARADISE

Hidden away in an unlikely subdivision in Coromandel Town is Greenhills Paradise, a small urban permaculture food forest designed to provide a diverse food source for bees, birds and Jo's family. Working with nature rather than against it, she has transformed an unremarkable back lawn into an astonishing array of fruit trees, berries and vegetables, complete with chooks and quails.

Within the modest 200-square-metre patch you'll find apricots, plums, apples, pears, avocados, bananas, citrus, grapes, unusual berries such as the highly nutritious aronia berries (chokeberries) and juneberries (Canadian serviceberries) — as well as the more traditional black, red and white currants, raspberries, boysenberries, blackberries and strawberries. Filling the 'forest floor' is every type of herb and annual vegetable crop you can imagine, along with perennial vegetables such as Chinese, Jerusalem and globe artichokes. The polyculture Jo has achieved in this average-sized back yard is nothing short of remarkable.

When she's not spending time in her garden, Jo loves to preserve and ferment her produce. She has also started her own business, advising people on how to start their own food forest.

Avant-garde film maker and gardener Derek Jarman once said, 'Paradise haunts gardens, and some gardens are paradise.' . . . When people garden they create their own paradise; they organise nature in particular ways; they carve out space from whatever lies beyond the enclosure they have made. This is true even when the garden is but a few pots of geraniums or herbs on a terrace.

— MATT MORRIS, *COMMON GROUND: GARDEN HISTORIES OF AOTEAROA*

ABOUT THE GARDENER

Every year, Jo's father dug some very early potatoes from the garden for her brother's birthday in late October. They grew under the eaves of their suburban Kirikiriroa Hamilton house on a large section at the edge of a wide gully. The garden had just two fruit trees — a lemon and a golden delicious apple — and Jo's father had no interest in growing flowers beyond the odd companion plant. Vegetables were his obsession. Jo's mother had no interest in gardening but happily prepared, preserved and pickled the harvest.

On Saturdays, Jo much preferred helping her father in the garden than doing indoor chores.

The garden was a self-sufficient system that included composting, leaf mould and growing green crops — usually lupins — to be dug in each spring. Two protected 100-year-old oak trees provided Jo's pocket money: a cent for every pound of acorns collected off the lawn. Jo and her brother raked and shovelled acorns while their father sat on the porch steps with his scales at the ready.

A gap in the fence provided access to another world. The neighbour's glasshouse was right up against fence, and Jo liked to escape into the warm, humid garden that was such a contrast to her father's vegetable empire. Through the glass sliding doors of this massive glasshouse were hoyas, begonias, orchids and maidenhair ferns. It was brimming with exotic tropical plants and, to little Jo, it was a place of utter magic.

She remembers the lichen-encrusted wishing well next to the glasshouse, with its little bucket and crank-handle — there were certainly no mystical ornamental features in her own garden!

Jo has always gardened. During nursing school it was pots on windowsills and tomatoes and lettuces down the side of her flats. She's always composted, too — even in her flatting days — incapable of discarding even a potato skin into landfill. As a young solo mother of three daughters in Te Kauwhata she found time to garden while the girls were at school, and kept a garden as big as she could manage. It had rambling roses and hollyhocks at the street front, a vegetable garden down the side of the house, and an orchard and chickens out the back.

Around this time, Jo's friends Jeanette and Noel built a garden in Morrinsville that would prove to be a turning point for her, seeding an ambition that would come to fruition several years later. Their extensive kitchen garden grew enough to feed them and their family, with more still to share. Jo marvelled at the garden. She loved the idea of being self-sustainable.

She had loved the 1970s BBC sitcom *The Good Life*, in which Tom and Barbara quit the rat-race to convert their suburban garden into a self-sustainable mini-farm, so the concept wasn't new to Jo. She knew it was something she wanted to do, but also that she'd do it a bit differently. Watching her friends plough the rows with a rotary hoe, Jo was keen to garden in a way that replicated, and supported, natural processes.

After her children left home, Jo went to work on a herb farm in Te Kauwhata. It was a commercial-scale garden, but Jo loved spending her days among the fragrant herbs, brushing past them all day along the farm's wood-chip paths.

The Good Life never far from her mind, Jo had always dabbled with self-sufficiency and an organic way of life. A food forest was her dream, but she had to have the right property, and frankly, it was a daunting ambition: she didn't know where to start. She experimented with planting an organic orchard but it became so overgrown with weeds she felt like giving up. She watched *Maggie's Garden Show* religiously in the 1990s, following Maggie Barry along to gardens around Aotearoa. Long-running rural-life documentary series *Country Calendar* and RNZ's Sunday morning *Country Life* programme are also longstanding rituals.

Then when Jo and husband Sandy retired to Coromandel to be close to her daughters and grandchildren, things finally came together: she had enough time, a lot of knowledge and the right kind of property. She also had access to woodchip.

ABOUT THE GARDEN

Jo and Sandy moved to Coromandel Town in 2019. At 850 square metres it's the smallest property she's ever owned, and the extent of the garden was four fruit trees, a hedge and a lot of lawn. When Jo removed the swimming pool from the back lawn, the circular patch of bare soil was the perfect spot to try building the *hügelkultur* (mound bed) patch she had always wanted. But the mound looked a little out of place on its own so she built another one next to it. Then another.

During the Covid-19 lockdowns that began soon after they moved in, Jo discovered a Facebook page called 'Grow Food Not Lawns', and everything clicked into place. Jo's *hügelkultur* experiments multiplied and she began planting fruit trees. Having discovered that woodchip was brilliant for suppressing weeds, retaining moisture and building soil, she no longer faced the challenges that had defeated her earlier efforts. All the time she was learning: reading everything from the *Yates Garden Guide* to Kay Baxter's *Koanga Garden Guide* and watching practical demonstrations on YouTube.

She's never had a garden plan as such, but a guiding set of principles — organic gardening, sustainability, feeding themselves, feeding the birds and insects. She's always harboured a desire to go back to basics and prepare things from scratch, be it using fire to heat your home and water, or growing your own food to cook and preserve. Knowing where her food comes from and how it has grown is deeply important to Jo. Her food forest produce is nutritionally dense without pesticide or herbicide contamination. She believes that, in the long term, commercial agriculture will not be sufficient to support the world's burgeoning population, so it's more vital than ever to practise and share knowledge of food security.

The seven layers of the food forest, built on the mounds, are canopy trees, a lower tree layer, a shrub layer, a herb layer, the soil surface, roots and a vertical layer. Details of the enormously diverse plantings within each layer appear later in this chapter.

This diversity of species, as well as creating healthy, nutrient-dense soil, is key to this garden flourishing as a self-sustaining ecosystem. Prior to being subdivided and flattened with topsoil, the area was farmland that included a quarry. Stone had been dumped around the farm, which along with clay provides Jo with a mineral-rich but hard and rocky base. She had to use a crowbar to break up the rock to plant her fruit trees. She has since built up over a foot of soil through generous woodchip mulching, adding loads of homemade compost, and leaving any pruned or removed plant material in situ. The nitrogen source (greens) combined with the carbon source (browns) has produced valuable biomass, building up the soil by replicating natural processes.

Natives support Jo's exceptionally diverse plantings of exotic, mostly deciduous trees and shrubs. They include kānuka, mānuka, tītoki, pittosporum, karamū and putaputawētā.

Jo has done nearly all the work herself, including wheelbarrowing load after load of woodchip and breaking up rocks with a crowbar. Sandy used to be able to build or repair anything but he has been living for years with neurodegenerative Huntington's Disease and cannot assist now. Doing everything on her own has been Jo's biggest challenge, and while she feels as if there are some things she hasn't done as well as she'd have liked, or as well as Sandy would have, growing an urban food forest from scratch is not a bad accomplishment. She still plants potatoes under the eaves, just as her father did.

When she was a single mum the garden was always Jo's place of peace, a welcome contrast to the busy-ness of parenting three young children, and she now finds a similar peace in her food forest. In her own words, it changes her. In the garden Jo can be present with herself, with her achievements and with the stubbornness of seasons, forgetting for a moment the challenges of caring for Sandy.

It often takes an old photo of the garden, from last summer or the one before, for Jo to recognise the progress she has made. Her future plans for Greenhills Paradise are modest — to keep feeding herself and Sandy, to watch the garden mature, to see her grandchildren enjoy it, and to share her journey with others.

NOTES FROM JO

FOOD NOT LAWNS

Here are some tips for turning your lawn into a productive garden:

- Start off small and slowly build on your achievements.
- Work to a plan of what you want where, including pathways.
- Save/collect corrugated cardboard.
- Line the lawn with cardboard and cover with a good 30 centimetres of arborist mulch.
- Make holes in the cardboard and plant trees and shrubs in the soil beneath.
- You can't plant directly into fresh mulch. Plant smaller plants by making more holes in the cardboard and soil, pushing back the mulch and filling the hole with compost or soil so the plants have a good base for their roots to take. Spread the mulch back on top.
- Be vigilant with plucking out any stray grass that appears through the mulch. Eventually the grass will die, robbed of energy and light.
- In time, the mulch will break down into compost and you can plant directly into it.
- Keep replenishing your pathways with new mulch, scraping off the decomposed mulch to put around plants.

I don't dig anywhere in my garden (apart from holes for planting). I feed the soil from the top, using compost and chop 'n' drop to build up a wonderful layer of humus without destroying the mycelium (network of fungal threads) and microbes in the soil.

A lot of the plants I grow in my food forest are 'dynamic accumulators' and nitrogen-fixing plants that are valuable for chop 'n' drop. Rhubarb is a great example of a dynamic accumulator. Its deep tap roots mine minerals from deep in the soil and transport them up to the surface where they are stored in the leaves. When the leaves are chopped and dropped on the soil surface or made into a liquid fertiliser, these minerals are given back to the earth. Tagasaste is a nitrogen-fixing tree that grows really fast, so it can be cut back frequently to add nitrogen to the soil.

I have several piles of compost on the go all the time. Two neighbours give me all their lawn clippings which I layer in the compost heaps and spread directly over the food forest. I also collect a lot of seaweed and sea grass and spread that around fruit trees and in the kitchen garden area. I make seaweed liquid manure and use that as a foliar spray regularly.

Once the garden is established there's actually minimal work — probably less than a largish standard vegetable garden that has soil exposed to the elements. After I first covered the area in mulch I went out every day and plucked any shoots of Kikuyu grass that dared show their tips. After a few weeks I won the battle and very few emerged. The thickness of the mulch layer killed off the grass and most of the weeds. Dense planting creates less opportunity for weeds to grow.

If you have used spray to kill the grass (and I strongly recommend you don't), you can progress with the same procedure — cardboard and thick mulch — but I wouldn't plant anything for a few months because of spray residue.

I used to love mowing lawns — those lovely straight lines and tidy edges gave me pleasure. When I was mowing, I could let my mind wander wherever it wanted to go. But increasingly I started to look at the lawns around all the houses and think why do we do this? Why do we feel we have to have beautifully manicured lawns? (Why do women feel they have to shave their underarms and legs?!) It always seemed to me the fight was on to have a better lawn than the neighbours.

I now know that mowing lawns goes way back to the English tradition of when a neatly mown lawn out the front of your stately home was a sign of wealth. It showed that you could afford to have a large lawn as decoration rather than needing the space for stock food. As humans we have followed this tradition for hundreds of years like sheep.

I wanted to grow nutrient-dense, spray-free food and the back yard was the sunniest part of my section.

Imagine a hot summer's day. Mown lawn. Sitting outside under a shade umbrella. Heat is radiating off the grass, elevating the temperature around you. Compare this to a natural 'bush' setting where cool earth, trees and shrubs provide food, shelter, shade and a habitat for wildlife. It's a no-brainer, really.

PLANT LIST FOR A SEVEN-LAYER FOOD FOREST

Canopy trees
Banana, avocado, inga bean, dogwood, apple, plum, apricot, peach, nectarine, pear, orange, mandarin, lemon, juneberry, quince, fig, nīkau palm, mānuka, mountain pawpaw, Japanese raisin, bay, loquat

Lower tree layer
Elderberry, aronia berry, dwarf peach and nectarine, senna, tree medick, red and yellow guava, tagasaste, camellia, jabuticaba (Brazilian grape tree), bottlebrush, feijoa, kōwhai*

Shrub layer
Raspberry, boysenberry, gooseberry, Worcesterberry, stinging nettle, artichoke, canna lily, yacón, Chilean guava, hebe, koromiko, blueberry, currants (black, white and red)

Herb layer
Dill, fennel, mint, rosemary, thyme, parsley, salad burnet, plantain, Vietnamese mint, tarragon, coriander, lavender, sage, lemon balm, lemon verbena, horseradish

Soil surface
Strawberry, violet, herb robert, creeping thyme, pumpkin, gourd, cucumber

Roots
Potato, Chinese artichoke, kūmara, yacón, Jerusalem artichoke

Vertical layer
Grape, kiwifruit, pumpkin, gourd, runner bean, cucumber, boysenberry, raspberry, basket willow, caigua, star jasmine,* geranium, clematis*

* *These three plants are considered poisonous.*

BUSH RETREAT

Looking at Linda and Nick's garden, spinach bursting from the ground and cape gooseberries dripping off the fence, it would be hard to guess their inner-city location. Pōhutukawa roots cling to their sloped section, kererū crash-land in red matipo and gangs of kākā visit the garden regularly. It is proof that creating a thriving edible sanctuary is possible even on steep, challenging, Te Whanganui-a-Tara Wellington terrain.

The pair bought their Wilton home in 1980. The property fitted two key requirements: it had enough space for a greenhouse for Nick, and a vegetable garden for Linda. The small house is surrounded by a hilly belt of green bush.

Ngaio and beech trees were already well established on a sloping grass patch by the house when they moved in. Less welcome were the gorse and blackberry bushes dotted across the property. A lone tin fence surrounded an abandoned vegetable patch, keeping out the northerly wind.

There was a lot of work to be done but the bones were definitely there, so they got to work clearing the gorse and creating their vision.

It wouldn't take long for their Bush Retreat to come to life. For more than 40 years now, the Wellington garden has housed multiple vegetable beds producing in abundance, a thriving compost system and hundreds of cacti and succulents.

*It seems to me that the natural world is the greatest
source of excitement; the greatest source of visual beauty;
the greatest source of intellectual interest. It is the greatest
source of so much in life that makes life worth living.*

— SIR DAVID ATTENBOROUGH

ABOUT THE GARDENERS

Dannevirke-born Linda has long been surrounded by the rituals and rhythms of gardening. 'I remember my mother's garden well. There was a huge orchard, and if you stood on a fence you could reach up to pick the best greengage plums.' Linda's mother always grew enough veges for the whole family. One aunt down the road memorably grew currants, and another tended a vegetable patch.

There were family rituals around the annual planting and harvest. Nitrogen-fixing lupins were planted first, and when they reached a certain height they had to be dug in, then the rest of the garden could be planted. Linda recalls a large pit in the garden that was used to store carrots and parsnips. Damp hessian sacks would be laid in the pit, the root vegetables piled in, and another sack laid on top. It was a makeshift but effective coolstore. When root vegetables were on the menu Linda would be sent out to get them from 'the pit'. Other childhood jobs included picking peas and beans. There was never a shortage of tasks on the sheep and beef farm she grew up on; her memories are of her parents always being busy.

Nick's love for growing comes from time spent with his grandmother and her cactus collection, which covered the shelves of her laundry in Petone. She showed him how to grow his own cacti as a child, planting different species in paua shells collected from the beach. He vividly remembers how magical it seemed for something to appear and grow.

He was fascinated by the sculptural forms of cacti and other succulents. Both Nick's grandfathers were keen gardeners — one would often collect cow manure from beside the railway line to make fertiliser to improve his sandy soil. He produced an abundance of yams, Nick recalls. His other

grandfather, a Gallipoli veteran, had an orchard with plum trees, apple trees and a row of gooseberry bushes.

Linda and Nick moved into a flat together in the early 1970s, shortly after Linda had backpacked around the globe for three years. They had met at Wellington's Duke of Edinburgh pub before she left.

They shifted regularly from rental to rental in those early days. Linda had become a passionate composter, setting up composting systems in their various flats across Wellington, and having to leave them behind with every shift.

They resolved to start looking for a house to buy. By this time Nick had bought a large glasshouse to house his cactus collection, and they didn't want to be lugging that from flat to flat. They found the house in Wilton and decided it was the one. Nick's glasshouse was dismantled for the move, and they only broke two panes in the process. He recalls that the hardest part was moving the giant lumps of timber foundation that the frame was screwed onto.

Nick's day job was as a geologist at the Institute of Geological and Nuclear Sciences. Linda has worn myriad hats, in education, in Parliament, co-managing a health foods store and as a contract gardener.

ABOUT THE GARDEN

In classic Wellington fashion, Linda and Nick's garden is set against a hill. The steep section is sheltered from the icy southerly but does receive the full force of the northerly. The garden is terraced, one set of steep steps leading to a flat vegetable plot and a collection of composting barrels, another set above it leading to Nick's glasshouse. The early morning sun is blocked by trees and a steep bank, but afternoon light pours into the garden all year round. The spinach, silverbeet, rhubarb and sage clearly appreciate its warmth, all growing well over knee height.

The soil has never been easy here. At the top of the garden, where the vege plot is, you can barely put a spade in the hill slopes — the dry soil is rock hard. Compost-filled concrete beds forming a potager — quite fashionable in the 1980s — were the solution they decided on.

Once Linda had designed the layout of the garden, she began the arduous task of lugging bags of concrete up the hill. She created four beds on the patch, each of which took a lot of compost to fill. In fact she used up all the compost she had just filling the first, so she layered up newspaper and tree prunings in the others, right to the top. A pathway splits her fourth potager in half, after she realised it would be tricky to reach the centre to pick her daikon radish with perpetual spinach growing around its edges.

Spring onions, parsnips, carrots, beetroot and a patch of self-sown coriander sit next to the silverbeet, the latter mainly grown for the couple's hens (Lavender, Blackie, Speckles and Freckles) to enjoy. Sorrel and parsley grow companionably together, near a row of sage. Linda picks sage most days — she loves to fry the leaves in a pan with a bit of olive oil and salt and just enjoy them as little chips. 'It tastes quite luxurious,' she says. The vibrant orange of nasturtiums' heads are dotted throughout the patch.

Her patch of purple potatoes used to be the bane of her life because once they're in the garden you can never get rid of them, she says. These days she's found a way to be more relaxed about their growing habits. In her book *Edible Backyard* (2021) Kath Irvine recommends just letting them take over a wild space in the garden, give them a helping of compost from time to time and resign yourself to the fact that they'll keep popping up there every year.

Linda is most fond of her tangy cape gooseberries, which grow at the edge of the vegetable garden. The golden berries are slightly tart with a tropical taste; the flavour has been described as a blend between a pineapple, mango and tomato. It's a competition between Linda and the hens though: the birds have been known to jump up to pluck them before they're ripe. They love them, but so does Linda — especially to make pickles and to put in asparagus salad.

Fruit is abundant in the garden. Boysenberry and strawberry patches offer their juicy orbs in season, and a passionfruit vine snakes its way through a grapevine. Feijoas fall off the tree in early autumn. The health of Linda's edible paradise is a testament to her compost — dark, rich and full of worms — shaded under the grapevine. Native seedlings like kawakawa and whau have popped up in between the potagers and coexist happily with her vegetables.

No fences line the property; the couple's aim has always been to emulate Wellington's relationship to its bordering bush — to coexist with and embrace its green surroundings. 'We have a house, a deck, a vege garden, and a great green belt of bush around us,' says Linda.

A mix of low- and high-growing natives keep out the wind and attract native birds by the flockful. Kererū utilise Linda and Nick's birdbath daily. One day one shot past Linda's head and sat on the edge of the birdbath for a drink; now he brings his whole family to use it. She cleans it out every day for them.

Linda's advice for beginner gardeners is to visit other people's gardens for inspiration. A walking tour of Kath Irvine's property in Ōhau on an open day stuck with her and her daughter, who now has her own garden in Taranaki. 'You can do a lot in a small space. Grow what you like to eat, watch it, learn from it and you can't go wrong.'

NICK'S GLASSHOUSE AND ITS EXOTIC INHABITANTS

The cacti in Nick's glasshouse wouldn't look out of place on another planet altogether. Barbed fingers outstretch as if part of a great hand, enticing onlookers with their sharpened points. They sit in a mix of terracotta and plastic pots, some towering over Nick with necks almost as high as the roof. Others are small and stout, firmly set in their rocky soil.

Nick finds everything about cacti fascinating: their form, their biology and their history. He has an encyclopaedic knowledge of their botanical names and natural habitats. Now in his seventies, he's been an active member of the Cactus & Succulent Society of New Zealand for 50 years, serving as its president in 2019. Society members readily share their knowledge and swap cuttings.

After his early interest in cacti was sparked by his grandmother, he returned to growing cacti years later in his twenties. Incredibly, his current collection includes some specimens that belonged to his grandmother: *Gasteria verrucosa* and orchid cacti still thrive almost 60 years on.

Many of his others he has raised from seed bought from local growers and international seed merchants from as far away as Peru and The Netherlands. Today there are well over 500 cacti and other succulents in this glasshouse. He uses the term 'other succulents' because technically 'cactus' only applies to succulents native to North and South America and the Galapagos Islands.

His personal favourites vary, depending on what he is studying or trying to grow at the time. 'There are a few kicking around that I'm pretty fond of that I've had for more than 50 years,' he says '*Beaucarnea recurvata*, commonly known as ponytail palm — I've got those growing more than 2 metres tall. And I've always liked *Mammillaria* — there's about 40 of them here.' An *Aloe speciosa* growing outside the greenhouse is close to 3 metres tall, and flowers in winter.

His most unusual species is *Gasteria rawlinsonii*, its presence undiscovered in New Zealand until 2005. A woman in Napier had imported them in the 1950s, before the days of tightened border security and approved species lists. History is as fascinating as botany for Nick, who was awarded a Queen's Service Medal in 2022 for services to historical research. He voluntarily recorded details of deaths and burials in Wellington for the first 50 years of colonial settlement. He is never short of a topic of interest.

NOTES FROM LINDA

SLOW COMPOST

I have three compost bins, each about a metre square. They were made by a flatmate in the 1970s when the advice was to have three bins: keep filling bin No. 1; turn and mix into bin No. 2; turn and mix into bin No. 3. That all takes too long and is too much like hard work!

I'm told that my method is cold composting — but I know that if I don't get the mix right it gets too hot and all the worms try to climb out! Anyway, here's my method:

1. Keep a bucket in the kitchen lined with paper and add all your vege scraps, crushed eggshells, tea leaves and coffee grounds, avocado skins, paper napkins and tissues etc. Keep the contents covered with wet paper.
2. Bag up weeds, any green leafy matter, grass clippings, spent veges (after the chooks have eaten the best bits and stomped all over the rest), and also any brown stems of the soft variety, such as rengarenga seed heads.
3. Tip the soggy contents of the full bucket over the area of the bin and completely cover this with the bagged green material. If you have no collected wilted garden material on hand you can use wet newspaper, wet cardboard or wet pizza boxes for this layer . . . or add them on top anyway.
4. Keep the compost bin covered to retain moisture. Black plastic works well — worms like it dark.
5. Layer by layer, slowly the compost builds. When the bin is full, lay wet newspaper over the top and leave it to mature. This can take anything from six months to over a year.

Tips
- The trick is to add just enough organic matter in each layer without making the bin too hot for the worms.
- Compost from my three bins is just enough to feed my vege garden. On the rest of my garden I use sheet composting (cardboard with mulch on top) and chop 'n' drop.
- When I prune trees I use the good-sized wood for firewood, twigs for kindling and the rest I cut into 30–60-centimetre lengths and lay them across the ground. I spread these prunings all through the garden — around my trees, through the rengarenga etc.
- What you take from the land, give back to the soil.

+++

CREATING A NATIVE BUSH 'FENCE'

New Zealanders, especially in urban areas, seem to be obsessed with fencing. We do have a corrugated-iron fence for wind protection in the vege garden, and a see-through fence around the deck for safety, but my challenge has been to maintain a bush fence around the property perimeter, so we're enclosed without viewing other houses.

In order to create a bush-hedge effect I cluster together groundcovers, juvenile trees and shrubs and taller trees. Here are some of my favourite natives that are easy to grow and easy to propagate from seeds or cuttings.

Groundcovers
Fuchsia procumbens (creeping fuchsia)
Arthropodium bifurcatum (rengarenga lily)
Pratia (Lobelia) pedunculata (a variety of native lobelia,
    with purplish–blue flowers)
Lobelia angulata (white flowers)
Leptinella traillii (Traills button daisy)
Libertia ixioides (New Zealand iris)

Trees and shrubs

FOR THE BIRDS

Sophora microphylla or *S. tetraptera* (kōwhai)

Coprosma robusta (karamū)

Coprosma repens (taupata)

Coprosma lucida (shining karamū)

Macropiper excelsum (kawakawa — great for pesto too!)

Phormium tenax (flax)

FOR COLOUR

Pittosporum eugenioides (tarata)

Myrsine australis (red matipo)

Dodonaea viscosa (akeake)

Hebe stricta (koromiko)

Aristotelia serrata (makomako, wineberry)

Solanum laciniatum (poroporo)

FASTEST GROWING

Entelea arborescens (whau)

FOR INTEREST

Dysoxylum spectabile (kohekohe) — this tree has a lovely leaf form and its flowers and seeds sprout from its branches. It was common in early Wellington — refer to *Wellington's Living Cloak: A Guide to the Natural Plant Communities* (1993) by Isobel Gabites.

LINDA'S GUIDE TO PROPAGATING SUCCULENTS

I propagate succulents to use decoratively in pots and as replacements in the rockery. During the first Covid lockdown I used propagated succulents to make a green roof for my letterbox!

I use recycled cactus potting mix and plastic six-pack seedling trays — that way I end up with 'plugs' of succulents I can transplant. I keep them outside on trays for ease of watering and moving.

My top easy-growing hardy succulents (by colour) are:

BUSH RETREAT

- Pink: ×*Graptoveria* 'Huth's Pink' (grows from leaf cuttings)
- Dark red (almost black): *Aeonium schwarzkopf* (grows from stem cuttings)
- Lime green: *Sedum confusum*. This sedum is so vigorous it's almost a weed, so in my rockery I keep it in the six-pack pot to contain it, and mulch around it. This also gives it some height, and as soon as it spreads too far I replace it with a new pot.
- Grey/green: *Senecio serpens* or *S. mandraliscae*; *Echeveria elegans* (clumps well, great for edging, grows from offsets). Large form: *Echeveria* 'Imbricata' (develops offsets you can propagate).

With this selection you can create edging for pots, circles, lines and mass plantings in different shapes.

THE LITTLE INSECT FARM

The word 'bored' has likely never been spoken by any family member on Melissa and Aaron's rural Taranaki property. There is no shortage of life and action on the 1.4-hectare hillside section, and no shortage of jobs to check off.

Picture an extensive tiered vegetable garden, a steadily growing food forest — and breeding quarters for 1000 mealworms. Add three kids, a cat, a dog, a horse, a pony, chooks and a goat and you have The Little Insect Farm.

The road to creating a thriving edible paradise for their whānau has been anything but linear, and Melissa and Aaron are the first to admit it. A learning curve has spanned more than a decade. It started with a piece of bare land the pair were not too fond of. Visiting the property now, it's difficult to picture the garden in its original barren state, with nothing but a handful of rose bushes. The rest was bare paddocks, with fencing right up to the house. Cows' hooves had eroded the soil right up to the back deck.

The difference now is a prime example of what patience, grit and an openness to experimentation can lead to. Now, it's all go. There are constantly vegetables to harvest, fruit to pick, eggs to collect. Lucas (15), Cohen (10) and Alinka-Jean (seven) are all keen helpers with their own area of expertise — from planting seeds to pulling out weeds and slug hunting. Food resilience and an appreciation for the outdoors are being passed on at The Little Insect Farm in the best way possible — with hands deep in the soil.

Know your garden dream before you begin. Tuck it into your back pocket for when you feel low or need inspiration to take the next step and the one after that. You'll get there. And it's going to be amazing.

— KATH IRVINE, *THE EDIBLE BACKYARD*

ABOUT THE GARDENERS

Gardening has never felt too foreign for this couple, who both grew up on farms (Melissa on a sheep and beef farm in Taranaki, and Aaron a pig farm in the Waikato). 'I remember everyone having some sort of garden growing up,' says Melissa. 'My parents were quite old-school gardeners, and still are — they use a string line to get their vegetables perfectly straight and a rotary hoe to work the soil.' She recalls visiting an aunt in Auckland who loved dahlias and hibiscus. There was no lawn, it was all flowers, and Melissa and her cousin were always in trouble for kicking balls into them.

Aaron remembers as a child watching his mum tend to a vegetable garden, growing about 500 square metres worth of veges such as spinach, potatoes, lettuces and cucumbers. His father was the manager of the pig farm, and his mother cooked staff roast lunches with vegetables from the garden. Aaron recalls being given his own little patch to grow seedlings, and being so proud of the broccoli he grew.

Melissa and Aaron both have backgrounds in science, and now work at the same school, Melissa as a biology teacher and Aaron as a science technician. Melissa's passion has long been education around sustainability. Prior to teaching, she worked as an environmental educator at Rotokare Scenic Reserve, a large forested hill-country catchment. Through this work she concluded that conservation education is essential to get people on board with protecting the environment. She came across fantastic people in the field and realised that the key was to facilitate the sharing of all their valuable knowledge.

The pair were friends for years in high school, then lost touch and crossed paths again in their early twenties. At least, that's how Melissa tells the

story — Aaron recalls being 'besotted in love from the get-go'. By the time they met again, Melissa had acquired a new cooking hobby. While studying towards an honours degree in zoology — tree wētā her area of speciality — she and her classmates were experimenting with a wriggly snack. They were breeding mealworms to feed lizards and birds and often had extras, so naturally, the *Tenebrio molitor* were fried up or baked into cookies.

'They're actually quite delicious,' she says. 'With the environmental and food security issues that accompany a growing population, alternative protein sources are so needed. We are living in a world where we have to change people's minds, though. I've definitely dragged Aaron along this journey of farming mealworms at home.'

Melissa and Aaron's first horticultural collaboration was a stacked tyre garden on a property they bought in Hāwera in 2009. On a tin fence that got hot in the sun, Melissa grew her first capsicums. Buying some land was always the plan. They owned horses, and their self-sufficiency journey grew around them.

It wasn't long before Melissa spied their current Eltham property on her drive to work. They arranged a viewing, but neither of them actually liked it much. The house was 'pretty awful'. It was north facing though, with a great view, and even though it was an incredibly steep section, they could see potential. A persistent real estate agent eventually sealed the deal in 2011.

ABOUT THE GARDEN

The productive garden at The Little Insect Farm consists of an orchard and large terraced garden (established soon after they moved in), several *hügelkultur* beds on a flat area beside the house (built 2020–21), and a food forest (a work in progress). You can wander through a grove of fruit trees and pick guavas, apples, peaches, plums and feijoas. Vegetables keep the family happily fed — from summer staples like tomatoes and courgettes to heritage potatoes, asparagus, choko and yams.

Recent additions include two more varieties of corn to be dried and used for popcorn, much to the children's delight. New varieties of pumpkin and zucchini are also in the ground. 'We're really excited to be growing borlotti and lima beans, in the hope of taking care of more of our protein needs, more sustainably, throughout the wintertime,' says Melissa. Cornflowers, marigolds, sunflowers and pansies bloom across the property in between various edible herbs.

Their seasonal growing beds are *hügelkultur* raised beds, in which crops are rotated. *Hügelkultur* has been used for centuries in eastern Europe, particularly Germany, as a way of creating a garden bed from rotten logs and plant debris. Areas for raised beds are marked out and woody material is loaded on top, finished with compost and soil, then left to settle. The rotting wood creates a fertile, moisture-retaining bed for planting. One of the beds is quite shaded so it has had extra organic matter added. It is then covered with a thick layer of sheep-wool mulch in preparation for winter crops such as brassicas.

The topsoil on the property is good quality and pretty deep in places, 15–30 centimetres with crumbly clay underneath. Before any planting could be done, back when they first bought the property in 2011, there was hard landscaping to be done — initially to get the erosion sorted and to keep the deck from falling down. They visualised a terraced garden when they first arrived, because the site was north facing and close to the kitchen. Melissa's workmates organised a working bee to erect retaining walls. Melissa was pregnant with Cohen by this point, and Aaron had his appendix out the day before the working bee, but they carried on and got it done. Neighbours helped plant the first fruit trees.

The food forest is a brand-new development. 'We couldn't have imagined the food forest when we first moved in — we thought we wanted to raise animals. We did get 17 sheep, but it was such a lot of work. There were emergency caesareans, we were giving lambs mouth to mouth, [and several] were in the house at one point,' Melissa says. They decided plants would be a whole lot easier.

The first stage of the food forest was building paths and steps to create access. The autumn they built their paths was incredibly wet but eventually they were completed, carpeted and mulched. They began planting their food forest in the winter of 2022. With access to free resources such as mulch, bamboo, sheep dags and manure (from neighbours, mates and Facebook Marketplace) they ended up achieving far more than they expected in phase one, so they just kept going. The food forest is already prolific, heading into its second year; they chop 'n' drop weekly to mulch and to feed the soil.

'We just kept digging and planting; I definitely over-ordered on fruit trees,' says Melissa. 'We had all these blueberries and currant bushes too and just didn't have the space. We've created 80 square metres of gardens just in the past few months.'

The forest layers are in their early stages, but are emerging. Herbaceous perennials that offer plenty of ground cover, such as alpine strawberries and valerian, grow around the roots of pear and apple trees. The fruit trees were planted in heat-treated pallets, which have encouraged their roots to stabilise the hillside and will eventually rot away.

Making their own nutrient-rich compost has been a key element. A 'humanure' system and grey water mulch basins keep the garden fertile. Melissa and Aaron are problem solvers, so their discovery that the septic tank and grey water drainage system they inherited were seriously flawed didn't faze them. The pair have now installed mulch basins to deal with the grey water, and converted to a composting toilet in the house. After months of research, Melissa says, they concluded that 'it's really the ultimate responsibility to take care of your own waste. It's a shame [more people] don't see it as a resource for gardening and are afraid of their waste. Our garden has benefited from it hugely.'

Then there are the mealworms. They are 'farmed' in a system of plastic drawers separated by life stages, and fed on a combination of meal flour and oats. For moisture, they nibble on apple and carrot slices. Melissa and Aaron plan to farm the worms on a commercial scale eventually, for both livestock and human consumption. They ordered a huge shipment of breeding trays from Europe and are in the process of building a shed and establishing the infrastructure. A freeze-dryer to preserve the insects and also produce from the garden is on the cards too.

As well as hosting visitors through Secret Gardens, The Little Insect Farm is a regular fixture on the annual Taranaki Sustainable Backyards Trail. Melissa and Aaron like visitors to see that you don't need to have a lot of money and resources to have a productive garden. And you don't have to do it 'perfectly'. 'You can live in alignment with your values and learn plenty along the way,' says Melissa. There is no shame in pausing a project or taking it in a different direction if flaws pop up. 'I think too often people see these perfect gardens and they think, "I couldn't do that," but we want to tell people that they actually can.'

In hindsight, the pair wish they had prioritised planting a shelterbelt to protect the property from the prevailing winds. At the time they were put off by the outlay required to buy so many trees at once, but they can now see it would have been a good investment. They also wish they'd had access when they were starting off to the huge resource available on YouTube. 'Homesteading' wasn't as popular back then, so there was a lot of guesswork and learning by trial and error.

There are plenty of future plans in the works for The Little Insect Farm (naturally). The dream is to join the terrace garden with their permaculture food forest through a passive solar greenhouse built with recycled windows. The chickens are hopeful their run will be extended — they've heard there are plans for a tunnel running right around the perimeter of the forest, offering plenty more space to scratch around.

But first on the agenda for Aaron: the insect shed.

NOTES FROM MELISSA AND AARON

HÜGELKULTUR — LITTLE INSECT FARM STYLE

Traditionally, *hügelkultur* beds are built as mounds using logs and other plant material, topped with compost and then planted into. As the organic material in the mound breaks down it provides a natural source of rich compost for the plants. The logs also retain moisture.

Here at The Little Insect Farm we built our large raised *hügel* beds from recycled corrugated iron, then tightly packed them with logs and prunings. On top of this we added whatever organic material came to hand — seaweed, woodchip, animal manure, carbon crops. If you want to plant into them straight away you can add compost and potting mix directly to this.

To add strength to our beds and stop them bulging at the sides we used wire and strainers. We also capped the tops and used metal flashing on the corners for added strength and to eliminate sharp edges.

FARMING MEALWORMS

Mealworms are an excellent protein source for poultry, pets and humans. They are the larval form of the yellow mealworm beetle, *Tenebrio molitor*, a species of darkling beetle.

Dry-roasting is the best method of cooking them for human consumption. From there they can be used in a number of ways: ground up to make a protein-rich powder to add to shakes or baking, added whole to salads, etc. Eaten whole, they have a nice nutty flavour.

It is important to note that people who have a shellfish allergy may also be allergic to eating insects.

If you want to farm your own mealworms as a supplementary protein for your poultry, pet fish or reptiles, or to eat yourself, all you need is a four-tier set of plastic drawers (available from any of the large hardware/homeware stores) and an initial population of a minimum of 150 mealworms.

There are various online mealworm suppliers, or you can buy through Trade Me or some pet supply shops (they are used as food for lizards). If you buy through Trade Me you should consider waiting an entire generation before eating the mealworms, so that you know exactly what they have been eating. They can be fed to poultry straight away though.

This system should be kept somewhere dark and warm, with a constant temperature of around 25° C.

Top tray: Beetles

The top tray will be your egg-laying area, where the beetles are housed. Cut the bottom out of this plastic drawer and replace it with wire insect mesh — the sort used in insect screens on windows and doors. You can buy it in rolls from hardware stores.

Cover the bottom of this drawer with a layer of bran/wheatmeal — this is the substrate the beetles will lay their eggs into. The eggs are tiny so they will fall through the mesh to the larvae tray below. Using mesh will save you a lot of time sorting through the substrate to find eggs, and also reduces the likelihood of beetles eating the new larvae when the eggs hatch.

Beetles live for about 3 months and lay 70–100 eggs over that time. They don't fly or bite, so they are easy to care for.

Second tray: Larvae

The eggs hatch in 5–20 days depending on the conditions, and newly hatched larvae are the best stage for human consumption. You definitely want to eat them before they begin pupating, after 8–10 weeks, when they will be around 2.5 centimetres long.

When the larvae are about to pupate they lie on one side, slightly curled inwards (starting to form a C shape). They become very still, though if you touch them they will wriggle a bit.

If you're growing them for poultry, they can be fed at any life stage (beetles, larvae, pupae).

To maintain a good population you want to allow 10–20 per cent of your larvae to pupate to replace your beetles — i.e. don't eat them all at once!

Third tray: Pupae

It is a good idea to separate out the pupae from the larvae and move them into a separate tray to protect them from being eaten by worms or beetles. They pupate for 2–3 weeks before turning into beetles, assuming the temperature is optimum. Interestingly, in the wild, the pupae stage can last up to 9 months, including over winter.

Bottom tray: Frass

In the bottom tray we keep the frass (waste), which looks like fine sand and has no real smell. We use a kitchen sieve periodically to separate out the frass from the bran/wheatmeal substrate in the top three drawers. We keep this in the tray for some time to ensure that we haven't missed any eggs or larvae, then we use it in the garden — frass makes an amazing fertiliser.

Care

As long as you maintain good hygiene with your setup, the larvae (mealworms) are safe to eat. Freezing is the best way to kill them.

There is a variety of grains/brans that mealworms and beetles eat. We feed them a mix of rolled oats and wheat bran, putting some into each tray. For moisture, we give them slices of carrot and apple. They also like potato and banana skin.

The key thing is to ensure there is no mould growth in the drawers, so change the food out regularly.

Once a week we do a sort to move individuals to the correct tray, and use a sieve to help with that. *Make sure you do this outside, as the fine frass can be an irritant to airways.*

FANTAIL AND FLAX

On an exposed hillside 400 metres above sea level in Manawahe, Bay of Plenty, is Fantail and Flax. The steep 1.6-hectare garden has been built over many levels on Tania and Llew's 700-hectare beef cattle farm. They bought the property from Llew's father in the early 1990s as bare farmland, stripped of life by decades of grazing. Tania started the garden 25 years ago, before they even built their house, while living in a caravan on site.

The scale and diversity of Fantail and Flax is astounding, not least because Tania has done everything herself. She now has a productive permaculture orchard, a Japanese-inspired garden, a woodland area and a large tract of native bush. Then there's an arboretum planted with exotic specimen trees for autumn colour, and many other garden 'rooms'. The distinct zones allow Tania the opportunity to experiment with different styles, techniques and plant types.

Central to her vision is planting for the future. Fantail and Flax is a legacy project that started with creating conditions for attracting birdlife to restore ecosystems and regenerate native bush. Alongside her myriad garden projects, Tania has planted 1500 native trees and placed a fenced-off section of native bush in a covenant with the Queen Elizabeth II National Trust.

. . . you cannot act well in a place, [Wendell Berry] says, until you have understood what nature intended for it: 'The nature of the original forest is, so to speak, "the genius of the place", which one is obliged to consult, not by human prescription but by natural law.'

— GEOFF PARK, *THEATRE COUNTRY: ESSAYS ON LANDSCAPE & WHENUA*

ABOUT THE GARDENER

It had never occurred to Tania that her garden was worthy of attention: it's just something she does. When she first visited the bare farmland in the early '90s she was immediately struck by the complete absence of life — no plants, no birds, no insects — and so Fantail and Flax began.

Tania was born in Waiuku and spent the majority of her childhood in Edgecumbe, just 10 kilometres away from where she now lives, and spent every school holiday with her grandparents in Thames. Grandad Hone had a large vegetable garden, which he worked on full time in his retirement. He grew every kind of vegetable in abundance, and many varieties of fruit, including a prized early kiwifruit, at that time called Chinese gooseberry.

Exploring the far reaches of the garden — the lichen-covered branches of fruit trees, the rock wall and nearby creek — was Tania's happy place. Grandma Olga had a traditional rose garden, but her real project was preserving the fruit and vegetables grown by Hone. Each afternoon she took Tania for a stroll around the neighbourhood, always stopping to look at gardens and sometimes pinching a cutting. Then, after their nightly seven-vegetable dinner, Olga took her into the preserving store cupboard to choose dessert. For Tania, the cupboard with its orderly shelves laden with jars of glistening fruit was like a cave of precious jewels.

As a young teacher in her mid-twenties, Tania had sole charge of isolated Tokomaru Bay School. Her friend and nearest neighbour, Leigh, lived a 45-minute drive away. She introduced Tania to organic gardening, and had the first raised vegetable garden Tania had ever seen, as well as flowers and shrubs. Tania would visit Leigh for cups of tea and walks around the garden, then be sent home to the schoolhouse with cuttings and seedlings for the

3-metre garden patch beneath the front windows of her cottage. This tiny garden was the start of Tania's own gardening practice, experimenting with Leigh's seedlings and the gift of her knowledge.

A few years later, on the farm's home block where she and Llew lived in a caravan, Tania began to plant trees. It was 1995, and they were still a few years away from building a house on the land, but those early trees lining the newly established driveway helped stabilise the steep, barren slopes, and would soon provide shelter from the strong cold winds blowing directly from Mt Ruapehu.

Tania's garden began to emerge from the stripped farmland as she planted and built soil, inviting earthworms and birds to Fantail and Flax. Harakeke grew quickly, further stabilising the hilly home section and attracting birds with its sticky sweet flowers.

The garden areas continued to grow alongside her children — the garden was a huge part of her parenting. Days out were trips to the garden centre, where her children would pick out plants for their individual gardens. There was never a road trip without seedlings on their knees and trees craning over the back seat on the drive home.

Distinct projects and gardens came to reflect Tania's personality and she was constantly brimming with new ideas, running headlong into them. A trip to England in 2011 with her two daughters, then eight and 12, was a turning point. With her sister in tow, also a keen gardener, Tania's month-long family holiday was defined by garden visits. She was inspired by how these grand gardens flowed, each distinct area connected to the others, creating a cohesive whole. The revelation of how her gardening projects could better fit together as a whole, of 'gardening to the edges', has informed the now holistically integrated garden of Fantail and Flax.

Tania fastidiously maintained journals during this trip, keeping garden brochures and making copious notes. A self-described 'active relaxer', when she is not in the garden — or managing their farm and quarry — Tania is likely to be drawing plans, noting progress, recording plant names, describing her experiences in the garden, and researching. This record-keeping is an anchor to Tania's gardening — a way for her to keep track of what she's done when, organise her ambitious plans, and reflect on her work. Most of this paperwork is done in the early pre-dawn hours before her work day begins.

Her vision for the farm has always been for it to feel like a park. Her father-in-law helped her build solid wooden rails to keep cows away from single trees they planted across the farm — flowering cherries, copper beech, claret ash. In her trademark style she planned this planting fastidiously, doing a lot of observing from the road and marking ridges on the map, so that the planting would lead the eye to the skyline, softening the edges of the landscape.

It's all a process of negotiation with the farmer, Tania's husband Llew, because despite the many benefits of tree planting, it does compromise farmable land. It was only recently, when completing the last of the rails that her father-in-law told Tania it had always been his vision to plant trees throughout the farm, but he never had the funds or moral support. Without knowing it, she has realised his vision, and recognises the importance of support and collaboration in progressing ambitious projects like this.

Just as the far reaches of Olga and Hone's garden constituted a place of peace for Tania the child, Fantail and Flax fulfils the same role for her as an adult. Even in the early days, amid the lovely chaos of three children, 'all that digging' was key to her mental health. She has enjoyed witnessing her vision come to fruition in the beautiful native bush, tūī and kererū in abundance.

ABOUT THE GARDEN

Fantail and Flax has been all about building an environment not just for its owners to enjoy but for all the birds, bugs and future inhabitants. From the start, the site presented myriad challenges: it's awkwardly steep, the soil was impoverished by decades of intensive farming, it is right in the line of strong cold southerlies and, often trapped in cloud, it's always a few degrees colder than down on the flat.

Initially Tania planted 150 pine trees and a number of *Rudbeckia laciniata* (coneflower) — fast-growing species that would provide temporary shelter to enable the establishment of native planting. It was also immediately clear that making compost would be essential. Digging the rock-hard soil just wasn't physically possible, so no-dig gardening was born out of necessity. She makes her own compost with horse manure, chipped garden waste and well-rotted sheep manure from the old woolshed. She also buys in a chicken manure and mulch mix.

Today, Fantail and Flax's gardens include a 'hot garden' for warm-coloured flowers, dahlias and cannas, bordered by buxus hedges; a no-dig vegetable garden with espaliered fruit trees; an orchard in which Tania is currently companion-planting guilds of berries, herbs and flowers underneath her 20 fruit trees; an arboretum of 150 trees planted for autumn colour; an avenue of flowering gum trees; a bushwalk garden with a natural spring; two woodland walks; a marquee lawn bordered by cyprus and other conifers; regenerating native bush that was planted from scratch; a topiary garden; a Japanese-inspired garden and a cottage garden.

Native planting was Tania's first significant gardening project. It started with a pittosporum, planted in the early days when they were still living in the campervan. Bringing back birdlife was at the forefront of Tania's mind when she planted harakeke (flax) and tī kōuka (cabbage trees). Native planting in the bush area and elsewhere across the farm has been designed to create habitats with avenues to connect them, encouraging birds to follow the path.

All this native planting around the house had brought the birds closer. For years Tania watched a kererū swoop down low to the tī kōuka near the house, but never land. Recently, however, it came barrelling down to crash-land with a beak full of berries, and now she and her mate have established a nest close to the house. Birds, as well as being welcome on their own account, are vital to the establishment of native bush — their droppings spread fertilised seeds of plants they've eaten, enabling the process of regeneration to become a self-sufficient ecosystem.

Back in 2007, Tania organised a team of helpers to plant 1500 native tree seedlings in a steep gully on the property. Now fenced off, and with no intervention, this area has developed into established bush, generating its own seedlings courtesy of the abundant birdlife. Even within the first couple of years Tania was amazed by the amount of growth — an example of nature's ability to restore itself.

Most recently, on the edge of this native area, she has planted clusters of select species, displays that she hopes will one day help visitors, and future generations, more easily identify the native species. These include tawa, kauri, rewarewa and kahikatea.

Tania's third child, son Tom, was just six weeks old when she bought the first 40 trees for the arboretum — 10 each of four different species recommended by the nursery owner. She'd had an overwhelming feeling that she wanted some trees to walk around with Tom as he grew. With the abundance of native bush, the garden and farm lacked diversity of colour, so she decided on autumn colour as a requirement for the arboretum. They fenced off a section of the paddock with an electric fence and the arboretum grew from there.

Around this time Tania had been watching *The History of Gardening* on Sky and was inspired to learn about the work of Capability Brown and his approach to creating vistas in the landscape. This knowledge came to be influential in the arboretum design, as was her relationship with Bill and Ann of Tikitere Gardens in Rotorua. Exotic species selected for their autumn colour include oaks, cherries, Japanese and Canadian maples, ginkgo, liquidambar and silver birch. On the advice of Bill, each species has been planted as multiples in blocks, encouraging healthy growth and dramatic colour.

The arboretum is on a steep site which until recently had no walking tracks, so access for planting and maintenance was challenging. Tania carried the trees down one at a time, with a bucket of water in the other hand. When the tree was planted it got its only watering. Pruning is only carried out if a tree is damaged or obstructing a path, and any prunings are left under the trees to rot down and return their nutrients to the soil.

Tania walks the arboretum track daily, and from time to time will pull out grass growing around the trees. Occasionally she mulches them, but otherwise they're left to fend for themselves.

There are 150 trees in the arboretum, but across the whole farm Tania has planted thousands. She recently planted camellias at the bottom of the hill, hellebores under the birch trees and bluebells under the cherries to give a woodland feel. Her underplanting could continue but she's conscious of the need to stop, like an artist knowing when a painting is finished.

Fantail and Flax has been designed to thrive and regenerate on its own. If its future kaitiaki are not interested in continuing Tania's work, all they'll need to do is mow the lawn. Everything will just keep growing. Tania cringes at the green deserts that many farms have become and is proud of what she has created from the barren landscape. She's told her kids to scatter her ashes in the garden, and that if they ever cut down the trees she'll be back to haunt them!

NOTES FROM TANIA

TANIA'S TOPIARY TIPS

Topiary adds the most delightful structure to a garden. It provides a focal point, a pause, a formality to the simplest of gardens.

Over the years I have played with topiary with a variety of species. Mostly I clip into geometric shapes including balls, pyramids and domes — I haven't yet ventured into animals!

I have found native plants work incredibly well — especially corokia, akeake, griselinia and tōtara. Clipping the natives prolongs their life in the garden as it stops them getting leggy and unruly. The native topiary is planted throughout my garden beds.

I have carried out more traditional topiary — the layered/tiered variety — on *Buxus* 'Green Gem', *Lonicera nitida* (very fast growing) and *Eugenia ventenatii* (lilly pilly).

I started all my topiary from cuttings. Every year when I prune, I grow on any strong main-shoot cuttings. Or you can purchase any plant with a nice tight growing habit, preferably with a small to medium leaf and a central stem.

I grow topiary both in pots and in the garden. Some plants I grow from the start with the intention to have them as topiary; but sometimes I see an area that would benefit from the structure a topiary plant brings, so I topiary an existing plant.

Topiary step by step
- Select a plant with a straight/strong central leader.
- Follow the leader carefully with your eye, looking for the way the branches grow from the stem. The branches naturally form sets, coming off the stem in distinct tiers.
- Using sharp, clean secateurs or clippers, remove any branches outside of the desired shape. Be mindful that a branch you remove may affect the tier above.

- Clip the remaining leaves to form the shape you want — round, square, flat or whatever.
- Stand back, rotate the plant, look at it from all angles. Is it balanced?
- Take your time, clip a small amount at a time — you can always remove more but you can't put it back.
- Clip twice a year — in spring (once the new growth has hardened off) and autumn. They benefit from a light tidy-up in summer if growth has been strong.

ORCHARD GUILDS

A guild is a diverse, mutually beneficial plant community, a collection of plants that work together and support one another in a mini-ecosystem. My orchard guild is made up of eight layers:

1. Overstorey
2. Understorey
3. Bush layer
4. Herbaceous layer
5. Groundcover
6. Root layer
7. Vine layer
8. Fungi layer

The overstorey is the main large tree in your guild. In an orchard it is a fruit tree, such as a peach, plum or apple.

The understorey is a smaller tree. In my orchard I have added a new fruit tree of the same variety next to the overstorey tree. I have done this as my orchard trees are already over 10 years old and I want to have a new tree coming on. You could also use dwarf fruit trees.

The bush layer consists of any fruiting or flowering plant that forms a bush: currants, raspberries, blueberries, rosemary etc. These aromatic plants are known as 'confusers' — their strong scent distracts unwanted insects while attracting beneficial pollinators.

The herbaceous layer is plants that die back in winter: herbs, rhubarb, comfrey, yarrow. These are also nutrient accumulators, meaning they draw goodness up out of the soil with their deep tap root and make it available. Their broad leaves also distribute rainwater around the guild.

Groundcovers include strawberries, pumpkins and clover (which is also a nitrogen fixer). The groundcover protects the soil from the hot sun.

The vine layer can be anything you can grow up your main tree — a grape, cucumber, beans, tomatoes.

Add small logs to the guild to encourage the growth of fungi to augment the soil's biology.

These are the basic concepts and principles, but as with anything else in the garden, you can adapt these in whatever way suits you and your garden.

+ + +

CONCRETING 101

I have done all the concreting in my garden myself. I love the feeling of 'power' and accomplishment it gives you to be able to build something yourself.

As with any garden project, it pays to have a plan, and to have everything you need onsite before you start. Once you mix the concrete there's no time to stop, so have a cup of tea before you start!

To make concrete the ratio is 6:1 builder's mix to cement. Builder's mix is a mixture of sand and small stones and is available from building supply outlets. When mixed with cement (bought in bags) and water it makes concrete to use in projects such as garden edging, steps and paths.

To make mortar the ratio is 4:1 sand to cement. Mortar is the filling between solid objects such as bricks or stones.

First I make the concrete, using a sturdy builder's wheelbarrow to mix it in. I measure the quantities with my garden spade — 6 spades of builder's mix to 1 spade of cement. It's not 100 per cent accurate but it works. Mix together the way you would the dry ingredients of a cake. Then add water. The water will sit on the top of the dry ingredients so add a bit at time, stirring it in until it is the consistency of toothpaste. If you make it too wet, add more dry ingredients. Mix up a small amount in each batch, then more when you need it.

Depending on your project, you will need to have a support structure to pour the concrete into.

If you are building a low garden brick edging, prepare a shallow trench for the foundation of the edging, making sure you dig the whole thing before you mix the concrete. Use your spade to dig a trench about 5 centimetres deep. It should be wide enough to hold a single brick plus a little bit extra, so you can create a concrete strip in front of the bricks. I find it helpful to make this strip about the width of your lawnmower wheel — that way you can get a nice clean edge when you mow.

When building an edging I work in sections about 1–2 metres at a time. You'll need your mortar now too, so mix that up quickly in the wheelbarrow. Fill the trench with the concrete, lay a brick on top and tap it into place with a rubber hammer. Take the next brick and, using a flat trowel, wipe some mortar across the butt end of the brick, lay it on the concrete end to end with the first brick, and tap in place with the rubber hammer. Add more mortar to fill any gaps between the bricks. Continue this way along your project.

If building a step or something above the ground, you will need to prepare boxing. I have found offcuts of wood or sleepers to be useful, held in place by wooden pegs that have been sharpened at one end and hammered into the ground. Remove these after the concrete has set (in a couple of days).

To make your concrete smooth on top, you need to use a concrete trowel. Use the flat of the trowel to tap over the concrete to bring any water or air bubbles to the surface and cause the stones to sink. Trowel the watery surface back and forth to get a nice flat finish.

To clean up, once the concrete has started to set (go off), it can be brushed with a firm brush. This will remove any stray concrete from places you don't want it, such as on the bricks.

Hose down all your tools and equipment thoroughly before it dries.

ACKNOWLEDGEMENTS

Jane and Sophie wish to thank and acknowledge everyone who has helped create this beautiful book.

Firstly, a special thanks to the talented and inspiring gardeners who so generously contributed their time, passion and wisdom to this project: Phoebe and Dave Atkinson, Sue Davies, Violet Faigan, Melissa and Aaron Jacobson, Jenny Marshall, Lucy McIntosh and Jacob Sheehan, Tania Mischefski, Linda Morrison and Nick Perrin, Nicky Paul, Jo Sanderson, Ali Soper and Merve Yesilkir.

Thanks to our special friend and talented photographer Josephine Meachen — for your beautiful images, all those early starts and for believing in Secret Gardens from day one.

Thanks to Jenny Hellen at Allen & Unwin for your vision, guidance and encouragement, and your wonderful team who made every step of the process such a joy — Rachel Scott, Kate Grimstock, Katrina Duncan, Alice Duncan-Gardiner and Tracey Wogan. Thanks, too, to Nicole Barratt, Kerry Argus and Peter Bannan for your contributions.

Heartfelt thanks to our partners, family and friends for your unwavering support — especially Jo Standage and Steph Oborn, Margaret (and the late Maurice) Mahoney, Edith (and the late Les) Bannan, Florence and Oscar Bannan, and Harriet and Nick Sargent.

And finally, a huge thank you to all the Secret Gardens hosts, and to our growing, connected community of generous and curious gardeners, and kaitiaki of this whenua, throughout Aotearoa.

FURTHER READING

Alexander, Grace, *Grow and Gather: A Gardener's Guide to a Year of Cut Flowers*, Quadrille Publishing Ltd., United Kingdom, 2021.

Baxter, Kay, *Koanga Garden Guide: A Complete Guide to Gardening Organically and Regeneratively*, Koanga Institute, New Zealand, 2015 (revised edition).

Chatto, Beth, *Beth Chatto's Woodland Garden: Shade-Loving Plants for Year-Round Interest*, Cassell, United Kingdom, 2002.

Cluitmans, Laurie (ed.), *On the Necessity of Gardening: An ABC of Art, Botany and Cultivation*, Valiz and Centraal Museum, Utrecht, 2021.

Harrison, Melissa, *The Stubborn Light of Things: A Nature Diary*, Faber & Faber, United Kingdom, 2020.

Irvine, Kath, *The Edible Backyard: A Practical Guide to Growing Organic Fruit and Vegetables All Year Round*, RHNZ Godwit, New Zealand, 2021.

Jekyll, Gertrude, *Colour in the Flower Garden*, Home Farm Books, United Kingdom, 1911 (2015 edition).

Kellaway, Deborah (ed.), *The Virago Book of Women Gardeners*, Little, Brown Book Group, United Kingdom, 1996.

Morris, Matt, *Common Ground: Garden Histories of Aotearoa*, Otago University Press, New Zealand, 2020.

Park, Geoff, *Theatre Country: Essays on Landscape & Whenua*, Te Herenga Waka University Press, New Zealand, 2006.

PHOTOGRAPHY CREDITS

Dave Atkinson: Page 38

Peter Bannan: Page 318 (bottom)

Sophie Bannan: Pages 32 (top left), 78 (middle left, bottom left, bottom right), 79 (all), 82–83, 84 (middle, bottom left), 87 (top left), 88 (middle, top right), 92, 176 (bottom left), 182 (bottom right), 183 (middle, bottom left, bottom right), 188 (top and bottom)

Jane Mahoney: Pages 2, 6 (top and bottom), 9 (top and bottom), 10–11, 14–15, 16–17, 22–23, 24, 27 (all), 30–31, 32 (top right, middle, bottom left and right), 33 (all), 51 (top right, middle, bottom right), 52–53, 54 (top left, top right, bottom left), 58–59, 60 (top and bottom), 66 (bottom left, bottom right), 100–101, 108 (all but top left and bottom right), 109 (all but bottom right), 114–15, 116 (top left), 122–23, 124–25, 128–29, 132 (all), 135 (all), 138 (all), 141 (all), 144–45, 150, 161 (all but middle right, bottom middle, bottom right), 162 (all but second row right, third row left, third row middle, fourth row right, bottom left, bottom right), 163 (all but top left, top right, third row left, fourth row middle, fourth row right, bottom right), 166–67, 168–69, 172–73, 176 (all but bottom left), 179 (top and bottom), 182 (all but bottom right), 183 (top left, top right), 184 (top and bottom), 189, 198–99, 202 (all), 206 (top right), 207 (top right, bottom left), 211 (all but top left, middle left), 212 (all but top left, second row middle, bottom right), 213 (all but second row middle, fourth row middle, fifth row middle, bottom left, bottom middle), 236–37, 238–39, 242, 244–45, 246–47, 248 (top and bottom), 251 (top and bottom), 252–53, 254, 256 (all), 257 (all), 258 (all), 262 (all), 266–67, 268–69, 272, 274–75, 276–77, 278 (all), 282 (all), 283 (all), 284 (top and bottom), 290–91, 300 (bottom left), 301 (all), 306 (top left, middle, bottom left), 313 (top and bottom)

Josephine Meachen: Pages 4–5, 42–43, 44–45, 48, 51 (top left, bottom left), 54 (middle, bottom right), 64–65, 66 (top left, top right, middle), 72–73, 74–75, 78 (top, middle right), 84 (top left, top right, bottom right), 87 (all but top left), 88 (top left, bottom left, bottom right), 98–99, 104–5, 108 (top left, bottom right), 109 (bottom right), 110 (all), 116 (all but top left), 146–47, 152 (all), 153 (top and bottom), 154, 157 (all), 158 (all), 161 (middle right, bottom middle, bottom right), 162 (second row right, third row left, third row middle, fourth row right, bottom left, bottom right), 163 (top left, top right, third row left, fourth row middle, fourth row right, bottom right), 192–93, 194–95, 206 (top left, middle, bottom left, bottom right), 207 (top left, middle, bottom right), 211 (top left, middle left), 212 (top left, second row middle, bottom right), 213 (second row middle, fourth row middle, fifth row middle, bottom left, bottom middle), 216–17, 218–19, 222 (all), 224–25, 226, 229, 230 (all), 292–93, 296–97, 300 (all but bottom left), 302, 306 (top right, bottom right), 307 (all), 308 (top and bottom), 314, 318 (top)

ABOUT THE AUTHORS

Jane Mahoney founded Secret Gardens (secretgardens.co.nz), an online garden-sharing platform, in 2021. She is a casting director for film and TV, and an avid life-long gardener. Jane shares her one-acre Corsair Bay Ōtautahi garden with partner Jo and cat Pearl. She also takes care of an historic Canterbury cottage garden at Brookside, that has been in the family since her childhood. Jane is an advocate of biodiversity, food security, regenerative gardening practices and knowledge-sharing.

Sophie Bannan is a writer and educator in Tāmaki Makaurau Auckland, where she gardens a 3 × 3-metre allotment at Sanctuary Mahi Whenua community garden and writes for art publications. The allotment is a space for growing food, small-scale experiments and learning from its community of gardeners. Sophie has written for numerous journals and catalogues including *Ceramics New Zealand*, *McCahon 100* and 'Miranda Parkes: The Merrier' (Hocken Gallery).

First published in 2023

Text © Jane Mahoney & Sophie Bannan, 2023
Photography © individual contributors (see page 317), 2023

All rights reserved. No part of this book may be reproduced or transmitted in any form or by any means, electronic or mechanical, including photocopying, recording or by any information storage and retrieval system, without prior permission in writing from the publisher.

Allen & Unwin
Level 2, 10 College Hill, Freemans Bay
Auckland 1011, New Zealand
(64 9) 377 3800
auckland@allenandunwin.com
www.allenandunwin.co.nz

83 Alexander Street
Crows Nest NSW 2065, Australia
Phone: (61 2) 8425 0100

A catalogue record for this book is available from
the National Library of New Zealand.

ISBN 978 1 99100 624 0

Text design by Katrina Duncan
Set in Heldane Text
Illustrations on pages 35, 90 and 91 by Alice Duncan-Gardiner
Printed and bound in China by C&C Offset Printing Co., Ltd

10 9 8 7 6 5 4 3 2 1